MW00575377

GREGORIAN CHANT EXPERIENCE

For Nóirín Ní Riain, Gregorian Chant is an everyday happening. For many years she has had chants as intimate experiences, friends of the heart, to be sung and held close at times of joy and sorrow. These forty are her favourites – from 'Regina Caeli' to 'Pange Lingua', from 'Magnificat cum Alleluia' to the 'Gloria' – which have accompanied her through thick and thin, a source of meditation and healing. She shares this now, inviting you into her private space, in this collection of meditations, of performances and of beautifully transcribed chants, written in the hand of a modern-day scribe in the monastic tradition.

These heartsongs will tug the memory strings for many who learned plainchant as schoolchildren. They will introduce a young generation to what is for them a new experience. These are the religious songs of the ancients, now breathed into new life for our own time. They bear with them the wisdom and the serenity of centuries of meditation and attunement of the spirit.

Nóirín performs these chants sometimes on her own, sometimes with the gathering of student priests from St Patrick's College, Thurles. She accompanies them on Indian instruments – the surpeti and the shruti box – providing a continuous drone, sometimes breathy, sometimes plaintive, always anchoring the voice with an earthy sound.

**Through this book and recording, Nóirín hopes
you will share her strong sense of the special value of chant
by listening, singing, reading and meditating –
and letting these ancient chants soar.**

**THIS BOOK IS ACCOMPANIED BY A CD
on which all forty chants are sung**

Gregorian Chant Experience

Sing and Meditate with
NÓIRÍN NÍ RIAIN

Scribe
Dom Kevin Healy OSB

Overture, by Sinéad O Connor
Foreword, by Rev. Austin Flannery OP
Chant and Prayer, by Dom PLacid Murray OSB

THE O'BRIEN PRESS
DUBLIN

IRISH AMERICAN BOOK COMPANY (IABC)
Boulder, Colorado

NÓIRÍN NÍ RIAIN

Nóirín began to take singing lessons at seven years of age. She later went on to study music at University College Cork, specialising in religious music for post-graduate work. Alongside this she developed as a performer, focusing particularly on religious, Irish traditional and international religious music.

She has performed extensively worldwide. Notable events include: the International Peace Gathering at Costa Rica to introduce His Holiness the XIV Dalai Lama in 1989; the United Nations summit at Rio de Janeiro 1992; the European Cultural Month at Krakow, Poland 1992; the UN Earth summit in Copenhagen 1995; the World Women summit in Beijing 1995; she has performed in the Royal Festival Hall with Sinéad O Connor; with the American composer John Cage; with Markus and Simon Stockhausen; at the summer and winter solstice concerts in the Cathedral of St John the Divine, New York; with the Schola Gregoriana of Notre Dame University, Indiana, where she performed the leading role in *Anima*, by Hildegard von Bingen; she has sung several times in India as a delegate of the Irish government, and performed in war-torn Sarajevo.

RECORDINGS
Caoineadh na Maighdine, Good People All, Vox de Nube with the monks of Glenstal Abbey, *Stór Amhrán, Soundings, Celtic Soul*; featured vocalist on *Meditation in Wort und Clang* with Markus and Simon Stockhausen; *Illumination*, the Music of Hildegard von Bingen; guest singer on *Solstice Live* (Living Music USA) with Paul Winter Consort from Cathedral of St John the Divine.

BOOKS
Stór Amhrán, Im Bim Baboró

DOM KEVIN HEALY OSB

Has been a Benedictine monk at Glenstal Abbey for many years, and has a long familiarity with liturgical music – singing, writing, composing. He now lives and works in the monastery of Ewu-Ishan in Nigeria, Africa.

The student priests from
ST PATRICK'S COLLEGE, THURLES

See the List of Singers on page179. St Patrick's College is the Diocesan college for the diocese of Cashel and Emly.

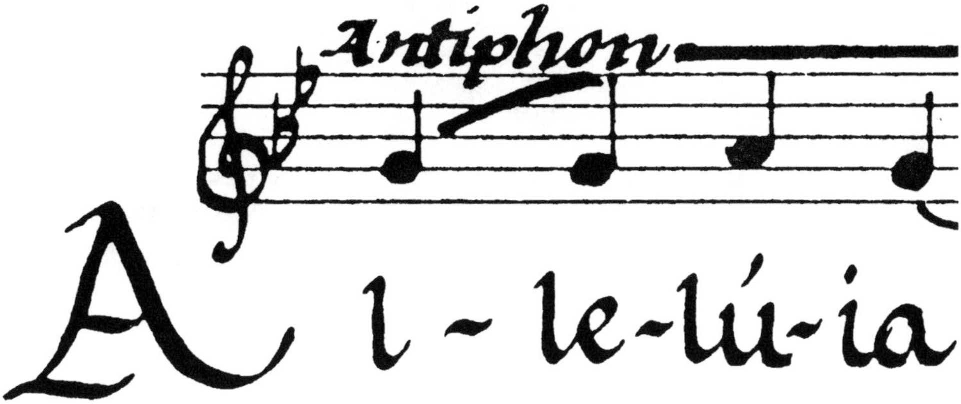
Antiphon
A l-le-lú-ia

First published 1997 by The O'Brien Press, Ltd.,
20 Victoria Road, Dublin 6, Ireland

Published in the US and Canada by the
Irish American Book Company (IABC)
6309 Monarch Park Place, Niwot, Colorado, 80503
Telephone (303) 530-1352, (800) 452-7115
Fax (303) 530-4488, (800) 401-9705

All author royalties from this book and CD go to THE FAMINE POT, a fund
towards the alleviation of children's suffering through world famine.
Details from: THE FAMINE POT, Dromore House, Newport,
County Tipperary, Ireland. FAX +353-(0)61-378793

British Library Cataloguing-in-publication Data
A catalogue reference for this book is available from the British Library.

ISBN: 0-86278-465-4

1 2 3 4 5 6 7 8 9 10
97 98 99 00 01 02 03 04 05

The O'Brien Press receives assistance from
The Arts Council/An Chomhairle Ealaíon

Typesetting, editing, design, layout: The O'Brien Press Ltd.
Front cover illustration: Aileen Johnston
Back cover illustration: from Marsh's Library, Dublin
Back cover photo: Jennifer Almquist
Cover separations: Lithoset Ltd., Dublin
Printing: The Guernsey Press Co. Ltd.

DEDICATION

Dirigátur Dómine orátio mea
Sicut incénsum in conspéctu tuo.
Let my prayer be directed, O Lord,
As incense in your sight.

Psalm 141

To Glenstal Abbey where I found my voice in chant,
and to all touched deeply by that sacred space

CONTENTS

OVERTURE

SINÉAD O CONNOR

How come that chanting and singing have been woven into our being since time began? It must be because singing is healing. I have felt the power of this in my own journey.

It's no accident that the voice is placed where it is, right between the head and the heart. Maybe that's why it can be difficult sometimes as a singer to FLY – when the head is dragging the heart down and refusing to let it loose and free. Also, the voice is halfway between the heavens and the earth – constantly grounding us to the earth at times then guiding our path up out of it at other times. While chatting and sharing singer-notes with Nóirín over the past few months, we discovered that we both feel the singer has two faces – like the Greek God Janus who had one head and two faces – one looking backwards and inwards and the other looking forwards and upwards. Song and chant places us in the 'between' – between heart and head, between the beyond and the here-and-now – pulling us in two directions. In this unity of opposites lies its healing powers.

The backward-looking, inward face is where your voice comes from, deep inside yourself, expressing your inner being in all its truth and vulnerability. Then the forward-looking face represents the listeners – the social side of singing, which has such tremendous power and potential for others, affecting everybody on some levels and a few in the deepest, richest way.

So, being a singer, performer or composer of deep songs in its own way is a huge responsibility – towards yourself, in maintaining those balances which allow you to share your soul totally, and also towards your listeners in drawing on their openness to this healing power.

When it comes to the Gregorian Chant before us here – one of the oldest forms of spiritual healing on the planet, the oldest songs in one of the oldest languages – a unique kind of healing power is possible. Singer and composer become anonymous and merge with the source of these songs which spring forth from the soil and the womb. Chant calls up a healing force of former people as a recipe for a contemporary cosmological cure for the chaos we all live through.

Peace and power within a world crying out for its own inner voice are what is happening here, and I am happy to be part of it.

Love,
Sinéad O Connor
London, 20 March 1996

FOREWORD

FR AUSTIN FLANNERY OP

The CD which accompanies this book is a welcome addition to the growing list of CDs of Gregorian Chant now available. The growth has been very fast. It was only in the autumn of 1993 that the trend-setting EMI-Odeón (Madrid) launched its double-disk album of recordings of Gregorian Chant by the Benedictine monks of the abbey of Saint Dominic of Silos, in northern Spain. It contained recordings made by the monks over the previous twenty years and was an immediate success, emboldening an American company to launch it in the United States the following March. There too, within weeks and to everybody's astonishment, this 'clerical chartbuster', as one reviewer dubbed it, became immensely popular. As its sales climbed into the millions, EMI-Odeón took to labelling their product the 'Original International Bestseller'.

Nóirín Ní Riain was into Gregorian Chant – indeed, passionately loved Gregorian Chant – long before many in these islands, or many Spaniards for that matter, had even heard of the Benedictines of Silos and the musical tradition which they had inherited from Solesmes, France.

For Silos is a small place in northern Spain, the sort of place which big-city folk label 'remote'. I had heard about it, in fact have visited it. Another Saint Dominic, the one who founded the order to which I belong, was born just a few miles away, in Caleruega, in 1170, almost a century after the death of the Silos Dominic, for whom he was named.

If I have gone on a bit about Silos it is because the antiquity of Silos – rebuilt in 1041 – is a reminder of the even greater antiquity of Gregorian Chant. And there is this too: Silos's choral and liturgical traditions serve to remind us that Gregorian Chant has an affinity with monasticism and that it is most at home in the liturgy, whether monastic or parochial.

This last should not be surprising. If the liturgy of the Western Church were a sensate, intelligent being it would express a marked preference for Gregorian Chant. Church authorities have long felt that, as the Second Vatican Council put it, Gregorian Chant is 'especially suited to the Roman liturgy. Therefore, other things being equal, it should be given pride of place in liturgical services' (Constitution on the Liturgy, 116).

Nóirín Ní Riain is fully aware of the close connections between Gregorian Chant, monasticism and the liturgy. She appreciates the choral tradition of the Benedictines of Glenstal, who have frequently collaborated with her and her husband, Mícheál Ó Súilleabháin, notably in the production of the excellent CD *Vox de Nube*. Not surprisingly, her book has managed to provide something of a monastic setting for the music of the CD. She herself has provided prayerful meditations on the chants, whose words Glenstal monk Kevin Healy has copied in a lovely calligrapher's script, an ancient monastic craft. Another monk of Glenstal, Placid Murray, out of long personal experience has written on prayer and Gregorian Chant. His essay is a reminder that, at its most authentic, Gregorian Chant is much more than a performance; it is prayer, and the music makes the words of prayer more prayerful still. As St Augustine said of a much earlier kind of chant, 'These holy words fill my soul with greater devotion when they are sung than when they are not' (*Confessions* 10, 33).

Nóirín Ní Riain is convinced that it would be greatly beneficial if some sung Latin chants were reintroduced into today's liturgy, and in this she is surely right. I think she will have achieved something splendid if her *Gregorian Chant Experience* helps to bring this about.

Not only would the inclusion of Gregorian Chants benefit the liturgy, however; the chants themselves would also surely benefit from being heard in their proper liturgical setting.

The English journalist Clifford Longley, veteran commentator on religious matters, made some pertinent comments recently in *The Daily Telegraph* (14 June, 1996) on the current popularity of Gregorian chant. He saw it as part of a post-modernist plundering of the past 'for styles and experiences, including (perhaps especially) the religious past' by a non churchgoing British public unable to connect in any real way with that past. He went on:

So the past becomes a theme park for the amusement of the visiting tourist. For instance, Gregorian plainsong (popular for chilling out after taking the drug Ecstasy, it is said) is now highly commercial. Record shops have shelves of it. But the truth about plainsong, that it is an ancient expression of collective prayer, is largely missed. This is one more illustration of the opacity of religion in a post-modernist culture. It is that very opacity that has rendered religious style and experiences now safe to play with – there is no danger of their underlying meaning taking hold.

Nóirín Ní Riain has gone to very great lengths to ensure that those who read her book and listen to her disk will be forcibly reminded of that underlying meaning. She is surely right to feel that somehow the time is now ripe for the introduction/re-introduction of Gregorian Chant at Mass, especially on Sundays. The vernacular liturgy is firmly, and rightly, in place. However, the addition of an appropriate amount of sung Latin chant would do much to improve the celebration of our liturgy and indeed to increase its appeal. If we clergy have doubts about the popularity of Gregorian Chant today, we should take a look at the recent charts. The fact that sales of CDs of Gregorian Chant now total several million must tell us *something* about contemporary popular taste.

This book and disk deserve a most enthusiastic welcome.

CHANT AND PRAYER

DOM PLACID MURRAY OSB

What is the magic of plainchant? How do you explain its sudden popularity among music lovers the world over? What makes it appeal to such a wide listening public? Will it be possible to reinstate it once again among choirs as a major element in worship?

I can only speak from a lifetime of monastic experience in our Benedictine community at Glenstal, where the chant is in daily use, particularly for the Office of Vespers, but also for the weekday Masses in community and for the Benedictus antiphon at Morning Office. Not only the daily round, but the whole cycle of the liturgical year takes its feel and colouring from this constant presence of the chant in our worship.

The spirituality of the chant is primarily a liturgical and community one. It is closely bound up with the texts of the liturgical year, and the spirit in which we sing these words is summed up by St Benedict in Chapter 19 of his *Rule*:

> 'Let us therefore always remember what the prophet says:
> "Serve the Lord in fear."
> And again: "Sing the psalms with wisdom."
> And: "In the sight of the angels
> will I sing a psalm to you."
> Let us therefore reflect
> what one should be in the sight of the Godhead and of his angels,
> and let us so stand at psalmody
> that mind and voice may be in tune.'[1]

These brief words open out before us an immense vista, where the actual musical performance comes in at the end, almost as an afterthought, that of being 'in tune'. It is not merely the voices of the different singers that are to be in tune, but the mind and voice of each single person present are to be in tune, in step together as the liturgy moves on. This is a discipline all its own, as the heading of St Benedict's chapter insinuates 'of *disciplined* psalmody.'[2]

'Mind' is what we bring to 'work' of God, 'voice' is what is offered to us in the words of the texts, which in almost every case come directly from the psalms or at least from some other part of Scripture, or scripturally related texts. Saint Ambrose has expressed beautifully this blending of 'mind' and 'voice' when he writes: 'In the psalm teaching is combined with charm; *for it is sung for pleasure but learnt for instruction.*'[3] Some further phrases of St Ambrose's from this same discourse on the psalms are worth recalling, since they express the spirituality of Christian psalmody, and hence of plainchant: ' in the psalms there is an opportunity for the people to bless and praise God; the psalms express the admiration that people feel and what the people want to say; in them the Church speaks, the faith is professed in a melodious way and authority finds a ready acceptance; there is heard the joyful call of freedom, the cry of pleasure and the sound of happiness. The psalm soothes anger, frees from care and drives away sadness. It is a weapon by night and a teacher by day: it is a shield in times of fear, an occasion of rejoicing for the holy, a mirror of tranquility; it is a pledge of peace and harmony, for with the aid of the harp the psalm makes one melody from a number of different notes. The beginning of the day hears the sound of the psalm and the end of the day hears its echoes.'

One of the great strengths of plainchant is its *repeatability*. This is an important factor in a monastic community where the daily chant has to go on in all weathers, at all seasons, and amid all fluctuations of health and moods. The familiar melodies awaken memories of former renderings, and so spur us on to appropriate them afresh. This is particularly true in the eighteen weeks of the great Church seasons, from Advent to Pentecost, each of which has its own particular flavour, unmistakably itself and not interchangeable with any other.

From the strictly musical angle, I suppose the repeatability has to do with the simple but subtle modal texture of the pieces, and with the basically straightforward tonic solfa scale intrinsic to them all. I can remember earlier years in Glenstal when we had little or no keyboard accompaniment to our Offices, and we managed very successfully with a tuning fork and a sense of pitch, singing *a cappella*, with unconscious memorising of the great pieces, and an ever keener entry into the modulations of the modes. We were more conscious then of the living unwritten tradition in which we stood and which reached back in unbroken succession to the first revival of Plain Chant under Pope Pius X.

The second great strength of plainchant is what one might call its *otherworldliness*. St Benedict's phrase quoted above speaks of our presence 'in the sight of God and of his angels'. This comes home to us when, as is frequently the case, there are no other 'spectators' at our Offices in choir. In fact, a guest recently said to me that the Office he appreciated most was our Morning Prayer, at which, by the very nature of the case, there can hardly ever be a congregation, except at high points of the year such as Holy Week, or the Vigil before Christmas Midnight Mass, or the annual Ecumenical conference. These Morning Offices go unrecorded, unseen, unheard, yet are carried out day after day to the best of our ability. Why? The answer is given, precisely for these 'hidden' Hours, in another phrase of St Benedict's:

'Let us then at these times give praise to our Creator
for the judgements of his justice ...
and at night let us get up, to give him praise.'[4]

As so frequently with St Benedict, he is here quoting a psalm [Ps 119:164,62]. What is at issue is the *laudative* character of the choral Office, and with it of the Plain Chant, which is like the perfume of a rose, so strong and yet so elusive. This praise is directed primarily 'to God and his angels'. This explains the feeling of constraint that we feel whenever we are asked to 'perform' whether on radio or TV or CD recordings. There is something unnatural in being lined up to suit the technical exigencies of such occasions, rather than sing away at our own accustomed pace 'in season, out of season.'

A further characteristic of the plainchant melodies is the *sonority* of the Latin vowels, and the *crispness* of the Latin consonants. Both of these come easily to us in Ireland, and in fact, an English Benedictine, a namesake of my own, Dom Gregory Murray, used to say that he never heard more beautiful renderings of the Latin plainchant pieces than those done by the children's choirs at the *Feiseanna*. The battle of the 60s about total intelligibility in the Church's language of her liturgy caused the eclipse of many beautiful Latin pieces of Plain Chant, pieces which are only waiting to be waved back into their pristine beauty, by a committed enthusiast such as the compiler of the present selection. We realise now that verbal intelligibility in liturgy is only one factor among many and although it is indispensable in the area of the Readings it is not the exclusive factor in the choice of sung pieces, where *remembered associations* go so deep.

This brings me to my final point: is there a *pastoral future* for plainchant in our liturgy? I speak as 'one less wise' on this, since my own experience (of 60 years!) is a monastic one. However, in retrospect, I now regret that in the days of the Glenstal Liturgical congresses, we withheld from promoting it, for the reasons hinted at above. I am glad therefore to be able to lend support to this new venture, to bring forth 'things old and new' from the treasure-house of the Church's live tradition.

CHANT AT GLENSTAL — A LIVING TRADITION

Plainchant at Glenstal is part of a living tradition, going back to the first years of the foundation of the monastery. This tradition in turn was part of a wider renewal of chant in the Church at large initiated by Pope Pius X at the beginning of the twentieth century. The Benedictine Abbey of Solesmes in France is the name most widely known in this field; however the house tradition in Glenstal, deriving as it does from its founding fathers from the Belgian Abbey of Maredsous, while using the Solesmes editions of the official books, was independent of the Solesmes interpretation and rendering, and was largely associated with the person of Dom Winoc Mertens, the earliest first chanter of our community. Other influences have played their part since the days of Father Winoc[5].

When the first group of Belgian monks came to found Glenstal in 1927, they brought with them a living tradition of plain chant from Maredsous, their mother-house. At that time in Ireland, plainchant was in a strong position in the schools as some basic pieces formed part of the Christian Doctrine syllabus in the primary schools, and was a constant feature at the Feis Ceóil, at which massed choirs of children sang the *Missa de Angelis*. This Irish tradition pre-dated the foundation of Glenstal, and was independent of it. Glenstal shared in this wider tradition in a modest way by the presence of Dom Winoc Mertens conducting the choirs here in Munster.

For the first two decades of its existence (1927-47) Glenstal's involvement in plainchant was mainly an internal community one, that of maintaining and nurturing – within the possibilities of the small numbers in the community – its inheritance in the Divine Office in choir and at the sung Mass on Sundays and great feasts.

It was with the advent of broadcast Masses that Glenstal made its first public appearance as a centre of plainchant in Ireland: the first radio Mass for the Sick on Radio Eireann in Ireland was broadcast from here in 1944, thanks to the invitation extended to the community to do so by the late Leon O'Broin, at that time Secretary of the Department of Posts and Telegraphs. Subsequently Glenstal was constantly called on to broadcast four such Masses each year.

The Liturgical Congresses 1954-71 emanating from here did not take up plainchant as one of its annual themes, although participation in the liturgy was a constant topic at the annual meetings. There was a feeling that the monastery should not encroach on the work of the parishes, although in the meantime, for whatever reason, the successful widespread 'school' plainchant never managed to get into Sunday Mass in the parishes.

The dates given in footnote 1 would suggest a broad division of forty years (1927-67) when the Benedictine Mass and Office chants at Glenstal were exclusively Latin and plainchant, while the following thirty years (1967-97) have witnessed the maintenance of these chants at daily Vespers, with efforts to incorporate or compose vernacular chants for the other Offices, and especially for the school Mass in term time. The monks have also recorded some cassettes and CDs of Irish music along with the writer of the present volume. The two TV showings of our Holy Week ceremonies also highlighted the fact that plainchant is a living tradition here.

1 *The Rule of Benedict, A Guide to Christian living.* The full text of the Rule in Latin and English with Commentary by George Holzherr, Abbot of Einsiedeln. Translated by Monks of Glenstal Abbey. Four Courts Press, 1994, p.145.

2 *De disciplina psallendi.*

3 Text available in *The Divine Office*, Week 10 of the Year: Saturday, Vol. III p.184.

4 *Rule*, 16,5.

5 It may be useful to recall some dates: Pope St. Pius X (1835-1914)

issued his *motu proprio* in 1903, restoring Gregorian Chant to its traditional place in the liturgy. The Second Vatican Council (1962-5) issued its Constitution on the Sacred Liturgy on 4 December 1963 which stated (Article 116): 'The Church recognizes Gregorian Chant as being specially suited to the Roman liturgy. Therefore, other things being equal, it should be given pride of place in liturgical services. Other kinds of sacred music, especially polyphony, are by no means excluded from liturgical celebrations so long as they accord with the spirit of the liturgical action as laid down in Article 30.' The second principle given here, together with the permission to use vernacular chants as *'liturgical'* chants, is the unintended cause of the disappearance of plainchant melodies from the popular memory.

PRE-MEDITATION

The genesis of any vision is always the story of a personal journey. Snatches of Gregorian Chant are scored into my life's memories. 'Pange Lingua' and 'Attende Domine' take me back to the heady childhood schooldays of overpoweringly pungent, incense-filled chapels at Benediction or school retreats. In those school days too, certain chants heralded in the seasons as powerfully and firmly as did the everchanging beauties of nature around me. Now as an adult, Gregorian Chant sings to and from my heart still.

A little girl growing up in Ireland of the fifties, I was bitten by the religious fervour all around. Going to Mass, saying the Stations of the Cross and the Rosary all colour brightly a canvas that was otherwise grey and dull. My deepest ambition was to be a priest and I practised every day, protected by the solitude and privacy of my parents' bedroom! After school, I would creep up there, lock the door and begin the ritual. Long before I knew what an entrance or recessional hymn was, I was crooning 'Tantum Ergo' at the beginning of my Mass and 'Regina Caeli' at the end, just before I stole out into the real world again.

'I'm going to be a priest,' I announced proudly to my brother, one day.

'Listen,' he hissed back at me, 'you can't even be an altar boy!'

The shock! It was then, at the age of seven, that I decided to become a singer. It was a unanimous decision between my parents, my teachers and myself. They said that I was always singing to myself anyway, so off I went to formal singing lessons. The so-called 'classical' style I learned then was to accompany me through thick and thin, for better or worse, from then on. There·were many, many thick and better times and I am always grateful to this tradition for those inspiring and inspired moments. But there were more thin times! Times when finding a voice, finding a repertoire seemed impossible; times of conforming, imitating; times of competition, nervousness, criticism, unease. After fifteen years, the marriage with classical singing was on the rocks!

The possibility of a new relationship appeared with Irish traditional songs – *sean-nós* – and particularly for me the traditional religious songs of Ireland. I fell madly in love! This traditional singing style was the perfect antidote to much of what I had turned against in formal, classical singing. I loved the total freedom of movement, voice, imagination, interpretation, meaning, which is the very centre of this, my own tradition.

The selfsame freedom of ecstatic possibility which I felt in traditional singing I also began to recall from a different type of traditional music – my memory of Gregorian Chant in childhood. I had a small repertoire of chant then which was to grow steadily over the years, a repertoire which enchanted me, and still does, way above and beyond any other music on this planet!

Each of the forty songs within these covers assumed a life of its own at some stage in my life's journey. For every single one of my forty years of singing these chants, I offer a chant now! Called into being and into their own space, these chants reside deep in my imagination and frequently summon me to sing them. Some fall very deliberately into the seasons and cyles of Christmas, Easter, Pentecost. Add to these songs dedicated to Mary, to Christ, chants of liturgy and loss, and you have the entire gamut of sevenfold themes of Gregorian Chant.

WHAT IS GREGORIAN CHANT?

Gregorian Chant, sometimes referred to as 'plainchant' or 'plainsong', is the large body of traditional melody of the Western Christian Church. Putting it in the Irish context, Gregorian Chant is the *sean-nós* of the Christian church! But unlike our own traditional music, it has been carefully documented and preserved through manuscripts, sometimes as poems only, where the music is a much later appendage to the prayers, and sometimes with the music-notes fairly clearly indicated in the form of neumes on the Gregorian stave. The textbooks tell us that St Ambrose, who died on the fourth of April exactly sixteen hundred years ago in AD 397, was the first teacher to have standardised the traditional music of Western Christendom. *Bis orat qui cantat*, 'the one who sings prays twice', was his motto as he praised God, preached and taught right belief through his popular hymns. I sing one wonderful Ambrosian hymn to the Trinity for you here (see page 88). As in any historical journey – sixteen or seventeen hundred years in this case – Gregorian Chant has taken many a battering; texts and tunes have been interfered with and adapted.

Now I could dazzle yourself and myself with the nitty-gritty details of history and transmission of the chant, but my concern is not the reproduction of facts. The story of my engagement with chant belongs to the realm of the intuitive. It's a story of emotion, firmly grounded in an ecological, holistic, direct relationship with existence rather than one of intellect or analysis. Mine is a 'hands on' approach, in the belief that an experience of actually singing Gregorian Chant is more worthwhile than facts and categorisations.

But for the reader and listener who wishes to gain a rational, focused, analytical overview of Gregorian Chant, I have compiled a Gregorian Chant Bibliography, listing those sources which I found the most helpful, though this is not comprehensive by any means (see p. 180).

A TRILOGY OF EMOTION – BEAUTY, LOSS, TIMING

In thinking about these chants there are at this very moment three burning ideas in my heart. First and foremost, there is the inexplicable, indefinable *beauty* of Gregorian Chant, its graciousness and reticence, which has to be heard, seen and sung to be believed. Hence the reason why we've chosen to present you with two media – listening and looking – in the optimistic hope that you'll give the third – singing – a try yourself to complete a trilogy of experience!

The second idea is one of *fear* and hovers around the danger of losing or forgetting this tradition, letting it slip like water through our hands. For me, it would be losing part of me, of what I am – a given tradition to be passed on, to be shared with others, with you. If this sounds arrogant, smug or presumptuous, I can only honestly and humbly say here at the outset that singing Gregorian Chant has thoughout *my* life been hugely transformative, healing and holy, and I firmly believe it can be for everybody.

The third idea has to do with *timing*. Timing is everything in life. Timing our relationships, our careers, our ambitions, our energy, our selfishness, our selflessness. And we very often get it wrong or seem to get it wrong. In retrospect though, we can see a direction, a tapestry emerging and often it's as if we're being guided. But if only someone could have set the alarm clock for us at the crucial moments! For me, the alarm went off rudely in my ear at least ten years ago when I awoke to dream a vision of this book and recording which you now hold. It's been one long day because the job at hand involved many other people to realise this dream – and that includes you. This is the time – the time for finding our spirit in chant.

> All one's life is music, if one touches
> the notes rightly and in time.
>
> John Ruskin

For me, having lived with and sung these chants through myriads of moods, ages and situations for almost forty years, to be suddenly thrown out on stage now not just to sing my song for the world but to try and express in words the depth of feelings this collective song brings, is a most important moment in my life. It makes me tremble with the excitement of sharing my vision of this wonderful music, but also with fear of the new, the added medium of words. Will I be able to call up for you the deep-felt moments and thoughts that lie inside attached to these chants? Shri Rama Krishna, the nineteenth-century Bengali Indian guru, once described the mind as 'a large treeful of noisy, chattering monkeys in constant chaotic movement from branch to branch'. As I write here, no other description seems to hit the nail on the head, to ring truer that this. My mind is buzzing.

Recently I was giving a workshop on singing and spirituality to a group of about thirty people in Limerick city near my home. Now, it was one of those days when I was full of the joys of life. I had been travelling and performing a lot, meeting new and stimulating minds, reading and listening avidly and generally feeling well in myself. As I drove into town, I couldn't help revelling in the fact of this day being an *average* Sunday when I would have the pleasure of sharing with people my song and story and they, in turn, would share theirs! The privilege of it all!

I began to speak and to sing. After some ten minutes or so, I became aware, as did most people nearby, of a young woman who was deeply, visibly moved, and the usual progression of the onset of tears was visible; the pattern of the first tears in the eyes, trying to fight them back, rooting in the bag for tissues, friend holding her hand and so on. In one space between my speech and song, she raised her hand to speak, more out of the need to break the obvious tension of the gathering which had built up around her, than from a desire to explain the tears.

'Listen,' she said, 'I have to tell you that the reason I'm crying is because you remind me so much of myself. You're all over the shop, off the wall in yourself, and I thought I was the only person in the world like that!' We've become great friends since!

So, let me reach into my many corners, off the wall or all over the shop as I may be, and try to pull out some treasures to share with you in words and in song. 'Tell all the truth,' said Emily Dickinson, 'but tell it slant.' Slant though it may be, I'll tell it anyway! To the rational, logical, organised, sober minds among you, I invite you to throw caution to the wind and jump into the boat I'm on for a few hours, a boat without oars, leaving ourselves to be tossed amid the unpredictability of the sea of chants or chance!

CHANTS TO SING – CHANCE TO PRAY

Trying to express in words the deepest of feelings is dangerous. Words mean different things to different people. So two images work well for me when I think of this trilogy of emotion – beauty, loss, timing – which I talk of above.

My first image is of a beautiful tropical forest. The diverse sounds and scents of life – throbbing, breathing, nourishing. I remember being overcome with the sense of awe, of Otherness, of God, call it what you will, in a tropical forest in Costa Rica. Every strong, graceful tree there, of which there are thousands of varieties, is a chant. The roots are hidden but delve deep into the soil and reach humanly untouchable, mysterious places.

So too with chant. It has sprung from another time, another people, another way of singing that we now have no access to, a sound only to be heard in the mind.

There is a tree in the forest there for all creatures great and small. So too, there is a chant which is waiting to nurture and sustain you and it is my prayer that you may find that one among this collection.

However, tropical forests are rapidly declining and have become an ecological world focus. Unmanaged commercial forestry is creating havoc through rampant deforestation. The balance between nature, climate and us human beings is being seriously tampered with. This is both a dangerous and an exciting time. Because now we know, now we have to take our place, sing our song for the earth, to redress that balance together.

Not wishing to detract from the gravity and magnitude of world forest future, there are parallels. Gregorian Chant forests have been slipping away too. Much of our chant deforestation is also due to mismanagement in the past, to well-intentioned but misguided efforts on the part of the clergy to integrate it into worship, often leaving a painful residue of memory for many people, including the clergy – chants being poorly taught and even more poorly performed; a total lack of pure joy, of cheerfulness, of playfulness that can still sometimes, unfortunately, accompany our liturgies and our prayers. On being asked about the cheerfulness of his Masses Joseph Haydn, the eighteenth-century Viennese classical composer replied: 'At the thought of God, my heart leapt for joy, and I could not help my music doing the same!' That joy is there too in Gregorian Chant, waiting to be rediscovered.

GIVE US THIS DAY OUR DAILY BREAD

The second image kneads the two remaining concepts – losing and recalling the chant – into one mental picture, and that is the symbolism of bread-making! Bread, like spirituality or chant, sustains and supports us. It is the staff of life.

Making bread, kneading the dough, can in itself be a prayer, a sacred ritual, binding itself in and through every culture and every time in history. Time was when bread-making, and indeed cooking in the home, was exclusively woman's world and territory. Change thankfully, for all our sakes and our sanity, has rapidly remodelled gender balance within the home to a far greater extent and pace than within the worlds of politics, business and religion. But that's another day's song! Nowadays, the image of bread-making is more inclusive. If you have never tried baking, here's my mother's recipe for brown soda bread, tried, tested and tasted for generations by the Hassett family of Birdhill, County Tipperary. So have a go!

COOSANE TRADITIONAL BROWN SODA BREAD
Ingredients
3 cups of brown wholemeal flour
1 cup of white flour
1 teaspoon of bread soda
A pinch of salt
Half a pint of buttermilk mixed with a little fresh milk

Mix the flours together, add bread soda and salt, and make a well in the centre of the dry mix. Add buttermilk and fresh milk and, with a wooden spoon, bind the elements together into a damp dough. Turn out on to a floured board or table, knead carefully, then mould into a circle, flatten the top and, with a knife, draw a cross on the bread face. Place in a fairly warm oven for thirty minutes.

The bread-making ceremony traditionally ends with sound. Every perfectly baked bread has its own hollow note, which is sounded by tapping the bottom of the hot bread.

THE STAFF OF LIFE

Three cups of brown flour represent three age-strata: young, middle-aged and older people for all of whom Gregorian Chant plucks at different heartstrings. Young people are mesmerised and spellbound by the exotic, indefinable nature of the power of chant; apparently discos and rave parties shift from being frenetic, sometimes uncontrolled nests of hysteria to motionless, ghostfilled caverns at the sound of the Mount Silos Benedictine monks of Spain. Middle-aged and older people retain Gregorian Chant just under the skin of their memory – people of my generation in their forties and over for whom religion was in the very air we breathed. Sometimes it stifled us, but at the same time it held us in readiness to be part of this new moment together.

One cup of white flour represents the male and female clergy and religious communities, who, despite the dwindling numbers and declining energy, will always be first-hand sources and custodians of chant. Indeed, chant could play a revitalising and stabilising role as the Roman Catholic Church treads the shaky path to the third millennium.

Bread soda and salt add the zest, the individual voice, which each one of us brings, the raising and purifying agents. These two ingredients, carefully yet haphazardly measured, seem to provide the ideal quality that defines the characteristic taste of each individual cake – the perfect blend of the masculine and feminine, the yin and yang of the bread!

The buttermilk, binding us all together, is the Holy Spirit, or indeed the spirit of togetherness, breathing peace and harmony upon all the separate yet combined components at this moment.

We are the needy, who pray and praise, and knead the dough as we sing the hymns together in that space where 'God comes to us and we go to God'.

The bread is marked with a cross, a universal symbol of balance and wholeness. For our foremothers this would have been a priestly ritual investing the merely practical with a consciously spiritual dimension. We bless the bread on its way to wholeness, and the miracle ensues!

It's done, transformed from a leathery piece of cold, lifeless substance. Through interaction with heat, with the divine, it rises ready to nurture and sustain all who partake!

We tap and listen for the muffled sound of completion and then together we partake, become companions (formed on the Latin words COM and *pánis*, 'one who eats bread with another') in chant!

High-fibre bread! High-fibre chant!

BRIDGING THE GENERATION AND THE VENERATION GAPS

Our two score, high-fibre chants here were recorded over three days in the chapel of St Patrick's College, Thurles. During the year when the seed of this collection was growing and germinating in my head, I made a few trips to the college to meet and sing through the pieces with the young student priests there. For an hour, we would gather in a circle seated on the carpeted floor of the chapel with a candle burning in the centre.

When the chantwork ended, the real work began! Long chats ensued, sometimes heated, sometimes hilarious. We covered everything from divorce to celibacy, from hurling to fashion, from mothers to smoking, yet a point always came where the significance of what we were about took over and conversation turned, as it does in many late-night pub discussions, to God and spirituality. With not a drop consumed by any of us! We were bridging gaps, building bridges. We were bridging the generation gap: there I was in the midst of twenty young lads, just a few years older than my own sons! We were aware at some level too that we were bridging veneration gaps: for my part, I was in the midst of these people who were living out and preparing for an even deeper commitment to the spiritual life, and yet I was introducing them to an aspect of their own tradition that they did not know. On their part, they recognised the timing in it all. Their openness, cheerful perseverance and trust in partaking of the goodies in the chantbag which I was carrying in on my back was astounding, yet real – chants they had never sung before, in a language which is no longer heard. Yet Gregorian Chant was an integral though silent part of their Roman Catholic tradition and legacy.

ABOUT THE MUSIC – SIGHT AND SOUND

Two traditional fiddle players in conversation:
'Can you read music or are you gifted?'

Well, music reading, music literacy can be for everyone and is within everyone to a certain degree. By that I mean we can all look at one of these beautiful work-of-art transcriptions here, and although many of you may not sing it straight off, there are at least three ways that you can become engaged with this chant.

You can like the look of a chant, rather like appreciating a painting. Though I know nothing about painting techniques, gazing on a work of art, not knowing even whether I like it or not, sends some extraordinary sensations racing through my blood and the memory often lives on for years afterwards. In these note-pictures you can see the up and down movement of the music, the architecture – the high and low notes as we inaccurately call them, because how can we say what's high and low in the vibrations of the miraculous vocal chords! You can match the line of notes with our singing, beginning and ending together with us, spotting the times when I, particularly, got carried away and began, unconsciously at the time, to sing my own Nóirínian chant!

The transcribing of Gregorian Chant evolved gradually over the centuries from little squiggles, which just jogged the 'off by heart' memory, to a rather complex system of square notes on four lines which is used solely for plainchant. Two voices in my head prompted me to transfer my chant selection from the original to conventional music notation, using the treble clef, and five lines and four spaces.

The first voice is the voice of the singer and teacher in me, who truly wants you to *sing* these chants – on your own, with the recording, with others in church, with others outside of church worship. Because each one of these songs is a song about God, a call to an unknown twilight. The unknown, the unpredictable presented itself in many forms as I put this collection together, and just as I had sometimes to stretch the words to make them fit, so too I indicate that stretch in the musical notation by the symbol – above the notes where notes defied timing and took their own pace. These chants are prayers first and foremost, not museum pieces, and are to be performed with the timing of the spirit.

The second voice is the voice of reason. This encouraged me to render the chants in readily recognisable notation, thus making it widely accessible.

Much more important was the presence of Dom Kevin Healy OSB, who I knew for certain was the only person in the whole world who would so sensitively step into the role of twentieth-century scribe. And because every written note and word would be a prayer for him, so too it could be and would be for us!

A sound-word here on the instrumental accompaniments you hear throughout the CD – the flavouring, the *bouquet garni* in the overall chant experience. Though never written down in medieval manuscripts there is evidence that instrumental drones ran continuously under chant, and I intuitively followed that tradition. A single, two-note reed drone of a fifth somehow seems to ground the chant on sacred *terra firma*, now supporting it, now poising it on vibrations from a similar sound-source. Interacting, playing about with each tiny interval between the billions of harmonics which each chant emits is what for me makes any plainchant touch that place of the near-perfect note.

So, what you hear now is no contrived, studio-doctored recording. Nor is it any definitive statement on how chant *should* be sung. We are all different, thank God! Different cultures, class, creed, different voices! In all areas of life, we find this one trying: coping with difference, with the Other in the other. Religion and chant have been no exception in intolerance and arrogance. A story from the eastern tradition reminds us of the value of difference. A beautiful falcon flies into the palace garden. The prime minister, a foolish man, sees the bird and having only seen a dove before now, he decides that, in all fairness to the falcon, he will have to step in and show him how to look like a proper dove. So he trims the wings, claws and beak of the falcon. 'Now you look decent,' he says.

Sing out with us with your own falcon's voice in a falconry of sound! Let no one interfere with that unique, one-off voice. If it sounds and feels good for you then it sounds and feels good to God, to the universe! Our recording is one gathering's honest, vulnerable prayer. Others will emerge with their own style. Like St John the Baptist we are 'a voice crying in the wilderness'.

Wearing the hat of producer, the only criterion employed in assembling the tape was a wish to capture the mood, the energy which accompanied the day and the time. I truly and wholeheartedly hope and believe we fulfilled this. Listen to this dome of sound which we created on that day, when like primeval stones in a circle we stood in a human soul-circle and took our place firmly in the tradition of our foreparents who sang plainchant in praise and thanksgiving.

From my story to yours! There are all kinds of chants here to behold and to live through, and, what's more, you can experience this collection in all kinds of ways: out on your own, to sing, to pray; with others, to teach and share; or just to observe from afar as a phenomenon, a curiosity. The choice is yours!

All I can say at this point is that each one of these chants has the power to bring us through the unknown twilight into the fullness of light – as the very first chant invites us, to 'dispel the clouds and darkness of the night', the night of our being. The very first sound you hear mirrors that pre-Christian, pagan ritual of greeting the first light of solstice from the darkness – from silence to sound, from dark to light.

Moving through this entire circle of chants is something like completing the cycle of human and natural experience. Each chant, not just within the span of its own sounding, but in perfect relationship to the others, calls up and challenges within us the presence or occasional absence of light in our lives. We will celebrate the mystery of our very co-existence and dialogue with nature together. And we do so above and beyond any particular institutional, religious denomination or background.

Beginning with songs of first light, of pre-Christian solstice time and of Christmas in later Christian terms, to a cycle in itself of seven Easter chants where we are guided gently, but firmly, deep into the darkness. But the third dawn awakens us from despair to unfeigned love and hope, to greet the other side of the light coin – the summer solstice. That delicate life-balance which confronts us all at one stage or another between the spiritual and the physical, the inspirational and the mundane then takes the stage through chants of specific function as we soar through Mass chants. The one and ultimate universal experience of death confronts us then through three insightful chants of Requiem.

Eight songs, which on the surface, seem merely to honour Mary from the Christian tradition, mean much, much more in this broader context. Here is an unwritten homage to that blend of Christian and pre-Christian, of masculine and feminine, of light and darkness in every human being. This cycle of Marian songs represents the one and only code to the combination-lock of life – the PIN number which gives just a tiny glimpse of the heavenly. Struggling for the correct PIN number is the challenge. A challenge which is continually changing and flowing, and which carries with it a dizziness and a confidence: the dizziness of looking up to the sky at a flock of homing pigeons just released to fly homewards; a confidence to swim out on your own, to fly out from under the wings of insecurity and fear with the voice of the heart and not of the head, regardless of what others might say.

As I struggle in that process myself, I can see us now as spokes of a great cosmological wheel of musical and peace-filled fortune which is being gently turned and tuned by the ultimate force above and beyond us all.

FROM
GODSONG
TO EARTHSONG

Veni, Veni, Emmanuel

V̌ E - ni, ve- ni, Em-má~ nu - el :

cap -tí- vum sol-ve Ís~ ra - el,

Qui ge -mit in ex- i - li - o,

pri~vá-tus De- i Fí ~ li - o.

℟ Gau-de, gau-de : Em-má ~ nu - el

nas-cé - tur pro-te, Ís — ra - el.

VENI, VENI, EMMANUEL

The maiden is with child
and will soon give birth to a son
whom she will call Immanuel.

Isaiah 7:14

Veni, veni Emmánuel:
captívum solve Ísrael,
Qui gemit in exílio,
privátus Dei Fílio.

REFRAIN:

Gaude, gaude: Emmánuel,
Nascétur prote, Ísrael.

Veni, veni o Óriens:
soláre nos advéniens;
Noctis depélle nebullas
Dirasque noctis tenébras.
REFRAIN.

Veni clavis Davídica:
regna reclude caélica.
Fac íter tutum superum,
et claude vías inférum.
REFRAIN.

Come, come,
Emmanuel: free
captive Israel who cries in
exile, deprived of the son of
God. Rejoice, rejoice:
Emmanuel will be born free,
O Israel. Come, come O
Dayspring, and console us in
your advent: dispel the clouds
and darkness of the night.
Come, O key of David, open
the kingdom of heaven: make
the path to heaven safe and
close the way to the infernal.

RORATE CAELI

See, the nations are like a drop on the pail's rim,
they count as a grain of dust on the scales.

Isaiah 40:15

ANTIPHON:

Roráte caeli desúper, et
nubes pluant justum.

Ne irascáris Dómine,
ne ultra memineris iniquitátis:
ecce cívitas sancti facta est
   desérta:
Sion desérta facta est:
Jerúsalem desoláta est:
domus sanctificatiónis tuae et
   glóriae tuae,
ubi laudavérunt te patres
   nostri.
ANTIPHON.

Consolámini, consolámini,
   pópule meus:
cito véniet salus tua:
quare maeróre consúmeris,
quia innovávit te dolor?
Salvábo te, noli timére,
ego enim sum Dóminus Deus
   tuus,
Sanctus Israel, Redémptor
   tuus.
ANTIPHON.

Drop down, heavens,
from above, and
clouds, rain down the Just
One. Do not be angry, Lord,
do not keep our failings in
mind: See, the city of the
Holy One is deserted, Sion is
deserted, Jerusalem is
desolate: the home of your
sanctification and your glory
where our fathers praised you.
Console, console my people,
your salvation will soon
come: why are you mourning
together because I will
transform your sorrow, I will
save you, do not be afraid, for
I am the Lord your God, the
Holy One of Israel, your
Redeemer.

Rorate cœli

Antiphon

RO-rá- te cœ-li de - sú-per?

et nu-bes plu- ant jus — tum.

NE i- tas-cá - ris, Dó — mi - ne,

ne ul-tra me-mi-ne-ris in-i-qui-tá - tis:

ec-ce cí-vi-tas sancti fac-ta est de-sér-ta:

Si- on de-sér — ta fac — ta est:

Je-rú-sa-lem de- so-lá- ta est:

do - mus sancti-fi - ca- ti-ó-nis tu-œ

et gló — ri - œ tu — œ

u-bi lau-da-vé — runt te

pa ~ tres nos ~ tri. *Antiphon.*

On-so-lá-mi-ni, conso-lá-mini, pó-pu-le me ~ us:

ci ~ to vé-ni ~ et sa ~ lus tu ~ a:

qua ~ re mœ-ró ~ re con ~ sú ~ me ~ ris,

qui ~ a in ~ no ~ vá-vit te do ~ lor?

Sal-vá ~ bo te, no-li ti ~ mé ~ re,

e ~ go e-nim sum Dó-mi-nus De-us tu ~ us,

Sanc-tus Is ~ ra-el, Redémp ~ tor tu ~ us. *Anti-phon*

MEDITATION

'Come, come, O Dayspring ... dispel the clouds and darkness of the night'
is the invitation *and* promise of our first solstice chant, 'Veni, Veni,
Emmanuel' – a chant of light to guide us on our way in this chant mystery
tour!

Advent – the four weeks before Christmas and the winter solstice – is the season for renewing and strengthening family ties, being familiar, going back home. Even our weather is telling us to stay in, to be warm, to spend the long evenings together! It offers an excuse to redress clogged-up relationships which may have become knotted over the year through selfishness, apathy, forgetfulness and preoccupation with oneself. So, as you listen to these Advent chants, think of people you need to re-connect with. It can take huge courage sometimes to re-visit an old friendship, to lift the phone and say 'How are you?' to a brother or sister from whom only time has distanced us.

Of all the yuletide songs my heartsong here is 'Veni, Veni, Emmanuel'. So I had to let it sound the first note and set the tone! The air is adapted from an eighteenth-century French missal, but the words, according to John Barkley in the *Handbook to the Church Hymnary*, come from the twelfth century. As I sang it for you, I couldn't help but repeat the final chorus – maybe you'll join in with me!

Calmness and serenity mark the musical and textual moods in 'Rorate Caeli', and I have felt this elusive stillness sometimes within myself as I sing through it. Two reasons at least for this, I'm sure. Firstly, the use of Latin – the mellifluous language of ancient Rome – instantly creates a composed, tranquil atmosphere, which I'm sure could be linked scientifically to the preponderance of open vowel sounds. Whatever it is, it's worth trying it for yourself. Just slowly say, chant or sing a few times: *Rorate caeli desuper, et nubes pluant justum.* Secondly, the integrity and honesty of the composer somehow shoots through one's soul like fireworks at midnight! This is a real prayer from the heart and no pious, contrived hymn. I chose the two verses here very deliberately. In the first verse, the praying one sings, begging God to overlook all failings. In the second and final verse, God takes over, promising to transform our sorrows, to allay our fears and to save us. The music beautifully complements the words, taking to the air in this final verse of Godsong. Listen to that little poignant phrase which through the music heightens the notion of sorrow: *quia innovavit te dolor.* Hats off to the anonymous composer who, in his or her genuine feelings of despair, created a healing medium for the rest of us!

Ecce nomen Domini

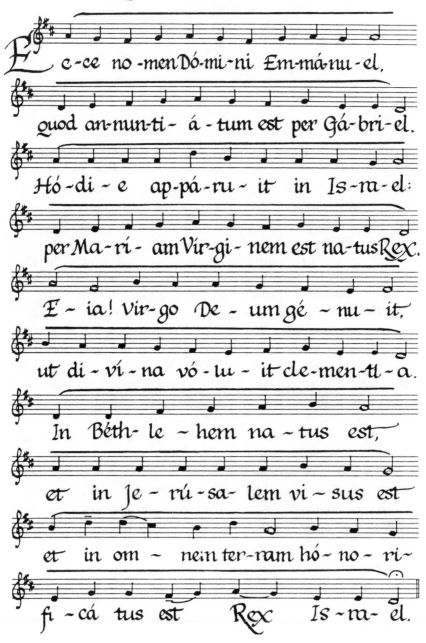

ECCE NOMEN DOMINI

The virgin will conceive and give birth to a son
and they will call him Emmanuel.

Matthew.1:23

Ecce nomen Dómini Emmánuel,
quod annuntiátum est per Gábriel
Hódie appáruit in Israel:
per Maríam Vírginem est natus Rex.
Eia! Virgo Deum génuit,
ut divína vóluit clementia.
In Béthlehem natus est,
et in Jerúsalem visus est,
et in omnem terram hónorificátus est Rex Israel.

Behold the name of the Lord, Emmanuel which was announced by Gabriel, today has appeared in Israel: through Mary the Virgin the King has been born. Eia! the Virgin bore God as divine clemency willed it. Born in Bethlehem and seen in Jerusalem, the King of Israel is honoured throughout the whole world.

MEDITATION

The name 'Emmanuel' sings a song of its own here as it welcomes us into a Christmas masterwork. Matthew, in his first chapter of the Good News, lights up this Hebrew name by telling us that 'they will call him Emmanuel, a name which means "God-is-with-us".' Our traditional Irish blessing to someone we meet: *Dia dhuit* (God be with you!) takes this Hebraical notion even further, becoming not only a blessing but a wish besides! A double moment.

As I listen here to this chant, another captivating, mantric word dances in my head: the Greek exclamation *Eia*. I love the way the music halts its jaunty pace just at this word to grasp our undivided attention for a moment, before resuming its former gallop once again! The English poet Geoffrey Hill begins two of the three poems in his wondrous trilogy of *Hymns to Our Lady of Chartres* with this very expression, which for him is strongly grounded in the evening chant to Mary, 'Salve Regina':

> Eia, with handbells, jews' harps, risible
> tuckets of salutation! Otherwise
> gnashing and gnawing sound out your praise.
> Salve regina! Visible, invisible ...
>
> Geoffrey Hill

I know nothing of the origins of 'Ecce Nomen Domini', an uncomplicated chant classic, but like 'Rorate Caeli' it feels unpretentious and sincere, and it brings to mind a poem by Thomas Hardy which I learned as a teenager. A poem that mingles the homeliness of Christmas with a passionate, quaint expression of love of nature.

> Christmas Eve, and twelve of the clock.
> 'Now they are all on their knees,'
> An elder said as we sat in a flock
> By the embers in hearthside ease.
>
> So fair a fancy few would weave
> In these years! Yet, I feel,
> If someone said on Christmas Eve,
> 'Come; see the oxen kneel
>
> 'In the lonely barton by yonder coomb
> Our childhood used to know,'
> I should go with him in the gloom,
> Hoping it might be so.
>
> Thomas Hardy

The Christmas Eve invitation to experience the Christian message of rebirth carries strongly within its memory an invitation to experience also the wonder of nature. The sun is overhead at the Tropic of Capricorn and for us in the northern hemisphere the day of least light has just passed. With candles – the perennial light-symbol – we invite in the New Year just as the Aran-islander Máirtín Ó Direáin in the poem below invites Mary into his island home. A candle in every window is the traditional Irish 'decoration' for Christmas, the light of invitation and welcome.

An eol duit, a Mhuire,
Cá rachair i mbliana
Ag iarraidh foscaidh
Do do Leanbh Naofa,
Tráth a bhfuil gach doras
Dúnta Ina éadan
Ag fuath is uabhar
An chine dhaonna?

Deonaigh glacadh
Le cuireadh uaimse
Go hoileán mara
San Iarthar cianda:
Beidh coinnle geala
I ngach fuinneog lasta
Is tine mhóna
Ar theallach adhainte.

Máirtín Ó Direáin

Do you know, Mary where you'll go this year, looking for shelter for your Holy Child; time was every door was closed on your face through the hatred and the arrogance of the human race? Accept from me my invitation to come to an island in the Western ocean: there will be candles lighting for ye in every window of my house and a fine turf fire kindling there. (Trans. N.Ní R.)

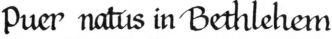

For there is a child born for us,
a son is given to us
and this is the name they give him:
Wonder-Counsellor, Mighty-God,
Eternal-Father, Prince-of-Peace.

Isaiah 9:5

PUER NATUS IN BETHLEHEM

Puer natus in Béthlehem,
    alleluia;
Unde gaudet Jerúsalem,
allelúia, allelúia.

REFRAIN:

In cordis júbilo Christum
    natum adorémus
Cum novo cántico.

Assúmpsit cárnem Fílius,
allelúia,
Déi Pátris altíssimus,
allelúia, allelúia.

REFRAIN.

Per Gabriélem núntium,
allelúia,
Vírgo concépit Fílium,
allelúia, allelúia.

REFRAIN.

In hoc natáli gáudio,
allelúia,
BENEDICÁMUS DÓMINO,
allelúia, allelúia.

REFRAIN.

Laudetur sancta Trinitas,
alleluia,
Deo dicamus gratias,
allelúia, allelúia.

REFRAIN.

A child is born in Bethlehem, alleluia. Wherefore Jerusalem rejoices, alleluia, alleluia. Cry aloud in your heart, Christ is born. Let us adore with a new song. The Son assumes flesh, alleluia. Son of the Father most high, alleluia, alleluia. Through Gabriel announced, alleluia. The Virgin conceived the Son, alleluia, alleluia. In this birth, let us rejoice, alleluia, let us bless the Lord, alleluia, alleluia. Praise the holy Trinity, alleluia, To God let us give thanks, alleluia, alleluia.

MEDITATION

Light looked down and beheld Darkness,
'Thither will I go,' said Light.
Peace looked down and beheld War,
'Thither will I go,' said Peace.
Love looked down and beheld Hatred,
'Thither will I go,' said Love.
So came Light, and shone;
So came Peace, and gave rest;
So came Love, and brought Life,
And the word was made Flesh, and dwelt among us.

Laurence Housman

The English poet and artist Laurence Housman, who died in 1959, weaves a daisy-chain of epiphanies here. In the depths of darkness, hatred and war, light, peace and love prevail.

Every time I sing this Christmas chant, the Easter chant 'O Filii et Filiae' (see page 74) hovers around. Both seem to draw from similar functional and structural wells.

On the functional side, the two chants let the final curtain down on the towering peaks of the Christian yearly cycle – Christmas and Easter. 'Puer Natus' is sung at the final procession of the Christmas vigil and the equally magical 'O Filii et Filiae' forms the closing notes of the Easter vigil. On the structural side, both draw at least three bucketsful, loaded with treasures, from a common well: one bucketful of Alleluias – three in both songs, though appearing in different patterns; a second bucketful of note-formations – both melodies are set in minor keys; and a third bucketful of verse-and-chorus patterns.

'Puer Natus' begins in quite an original way, with a verse not a chorus. It first appeared in a Benedictine processional of the fourteenth century, and was hugely popular over several centuries in Germany. And why wouldn't it be? Just experience the musical expertise here! The first two phrases rise out of nowhere like the sun, then disappear in the glorious musical sunset of *Cum novo cantico*. Actually, this little motif is a symphony in itself – a full statement, a sentence, a complete wish! I often sing it as a response to a spontaneous cosmic litany, which you can play around with too: Sing praise to the earth, *cum novo cantico!*

Christe Redémptor omnium

Christe Re- démptor óm-ni ~ um,

Ex Patre Pa-tris ú — ni ~ ce,

So ~ lus an ~ te prin ~ cí-pi ~ um,

Na-tus in ~ ef-fa ~ bí-li ~ ter?

A ~ men

My Lord, our King, the only one,
come to my help, for I am alone
and have no helper but you.

Esther's Song, Book of Esther 4:14

Christe Redémptor
ómnium,
    Ex Patre Patris únice,
Solus ante princípium
Natus ineffabíliter.

Tu lumen, tu splendor Patris,
Tu spes perénnis omnium,
Inténde quas fundunt preces
Tui per orbem fámuli.

Glória tibi Dómine,
Qui natus es de Vírgine,
Cum Patre et Sancto Spíritu,
In sempitérna saécula. Amen.

Christ, Redeemor of the world, begotten of the Father, light born before the beginning. You are the Light and Beauty of the Father, you are constant hope of all. Accept the prayers which your earthly servants pour to you. Glory to you Lord, who is born of the Virgin, with the Father and Holy Spirit, for ever and ever. Amen.

MEDITATION

'Christe Redemptor' is a chant which for me soars in sound, sight and sense. Two wonder-working lines say it all: *Solus ante principium* (light born before the beginning), and *Tu lumen, tu splendor Patris* (you are the Light and Beauty of the Father). These images take me back to two of the most inspired lines that my world of poetry has so far thrown up for me. They were written by John Keats, the great English poet of the late-eighteenth, early-nineteenth century. In the concluding lines of 'Ode to a Grecian Urn' he makes this one, great, universal declaration:

> Beauty is truth, truth beauty, – that is all
> Ye know on earth, and all ye need to know.
> John Keats

At the age of twenty-five, John Keats died in Rome from a throat illness and tuberculosis. Just nine years later, on the other side of the Atlantic, Emily Dickinson was born.

In 1990, between January and May, we lived *en famille*, for a five-month spell in Boston. For all of us it was a time of tremendous growth, carrying with it the attendant growing pains! Some of the pains grew from the dis-ease of homesickness, giving us a stark realisation of the plight of many of our poor Irish emigrant foremothers and forefathers who found themselves homeless in a foreign culture, a foreign climate. No bird-song there – I heard the first bird sing out over the snows on March the twelfth! Perhaps because of this long, hard winter, St Valentine's day was like Christmas for us, another time for giving and receiving. This was new to us. I spent hours during the advent to Valentinetide wrapping 'cookies' and cards for the little girls who shared school desks with my two sons. 'Pretty Sweeties' the little girls were called – but just for that day!

Well, my own 'pretty sweetie' that day presented me with a miniature collection from the New England poet, mystic and recluse, Emily Dickinson. Since then, no day goes down without some of her poems crossing my soul.

Her poetry is firmly intertwined with my own plainchant journey, and I cannot but share some of her words with you on our way. Could it be that Emily laid hands on a Keats collection which inspired her Truth and Beauty fantasy?

I died for Beauty – but was scarce
Adjusted in the Tomb
When One who died for Truth, was lain
In an adjoining Room –

He questioned softly 'Why I failed'?
'For Beauty', I replied –
'And I – for Truth – Themself are One –
We Brethren, are', He said –

And so, as Kinsmen, met a Night –
We talked between the Rooms –
Until the Moss had reached our lips –
And covered up – our names –

Emily Dickinson

The poetry of Emily Dickinson never fails to enchant me. Every one of the one thousand, seven hundred and seventy-five poems which she left behind has within it something of the Truth and Beauty which she so laboriously and fastidiously sought. You'll meet her again and again in my musings, not too often, I hope, to prevent you begging, stealing or borrowing a copy of her gems for yourself.

Nine hundred of these poems she herself carefully, meticulously wrote and bound with twine, choosing deliberately to leave them behind to be unravelled by us, her readers. Each poem demands that we handle it with care and untie the knot as delicately as she herself carefully tied it up with her precisely assembled thoughts. Pure Emilian chant!

So to match, heighten and close this Christmas medley, here's Emily's flight of yuletide fancy:

The Saviour must have been
A docile Gentleman –
To come so far so cold a Day
For little Fellowmen –

The road to Bethlehem
Since He and I were Boys
Was leveled, but for that 'twould be
A rugged billion Miles –

Emily Dickinson

THE
THIRD DAWN

Tertia lux rediit, surge sepulte meus
(The third dawn has come, rise up my buried one!)

Salve Festa Dies

The third dawn – that suspended moment between death and
resurrection, between darkness and light, the time and space of
possibility! A space undefined but there nonetheless, both tangible
and intangible – in Irish the *coicead*, the mysterious, non-existent
fifth province, the seventh heaven! Here, with these chants, let us
explore the mysterious spaces between suffering and exultation,
between denial and delight, between deliberateness and reticence.

Have mercy on me, O God, in your goodness,
in your great tenderness wipe away my faults;

Psalm 51:1

ANTPIHON:

Atténde Dómine, et
miserére,
quia peccávimus tibi.

Ad te, Rex summe, ómnium
Redémptor
óculos nostros sublevámus
flentes:
exáudi, Christe, supplicántum
preces.
ANTIPHON.

Déxtera Pátris, lápis anguláris,
vía salútis, janua caeléstis,
áblue nóstri máculas delícti.
ANTIPHON.

Take heed, Lord, and
have mercy, for we
have sinned against you. To
you, O Highest King,
Redeemer of all, we raise our
tearful eyes: Hear, O Christ,
our supplicant prayers. Right
hand of the Father,
cornerstone, way of
Salvation, gate of heaven,
wash away our sinful
offences.

MEDITATION

Here we are in Lent, that time of year between Ash Wednesday and Easter Eve, forty days which could be a time of possibility, yet were, in the past, too strongly coloured with stringent fasting and sometimes an overdose of doom and gloom! Yet I'm always grateful to have that memory in my soul. Nowadays, this time of Lent, which takes it name from the Old English name for spring, can be a time for balancing the unbalanced in our lives, for travelling inwards and upwards, taking stock, facing reality, starving the sin not the bin, as English poet Robert Herrick so cleverly puts it:

TO KEEP A TRUE LENT

Is this a Fast, to keep
    The Larder leane?
        And cleane
From fat of Veales and Sheep?

Is it to quit the dish,
    Of Flesh, yet still
        To fill
The platter high with Fish?

Is it to faste an houre,
    Or ragg'd to go,
        Or show
A downcast look, and sowre?

No: 'tis a Fast, to dole
    Thy sheaf of wheat
        And meat
Unto the hungry Soule.

It is to fast from strife
    From old debate,
        And hate;
To circumcise thy life.

To shew a heart grief-rent;
    To starve thy sin,
        Not Bin;
And that's to keep thy Lent.

Robert Herrick

'Attende Domine', this spring song, holds a paticular memory for me. When I first started teaching, I spent a year with the warm, motherly, Mercy community in Dungarvan, County Waterford. Full of enthusiasm, vision, exuberance and indeed little or no sense, I begged permission to audition every student in the school, with the goal of creating a choir of the most natural singers there. I selected twenty-nine girls between the ages of twelve and eighteen, and the authorities spared no generosity and support in facilitating two forty-minute periods a week when we could meet. I will never forget the sheer excitement through that year of sharing, hearing and singing all kinds of songs with them – songs which meant the world to me then: rock songs, folk, *sean-nós*, jazz, classical, Black spiritual songs and, of course, Gregorian Chant.

Well, in June of that year, knowing sadly that I was to leave in September, I ran a rather detailed though amateur survey among my 'friends', as they had become, since I was only three years older than the oldest girls at the time! Twenty-five replied that their favourite genre of song over the year was – wait for it – plainchant, and furthermore, that they felt physically better having sung a chant! This one , 'Attende Domine', was the best-loved of some twenty chants which had come alive for them, and over the suitable gestation period of just nine months together it birthed the idea of this book and the strongest possible conviction in the healing power of the chant tradition.

For me, there is no lovelier note-pattern than the first three notes on *'quia peccavimus tibi'*, made all the lovelier by concluding the phrase so satisfyingly in six more notes which sing like a sparkling waterfall.

In fact, this chant has an ecological feel to it, a wholesome balance of opposites. The chorus has two phrases, two statements. The verse, however, has three. Twos against threes. The two-phrased chorus seems to earth the three-phrased verse, and the see-saw delicately levels out in the overlap and silent spaces between both. Although it is impossible to say for certain what makes this chant more emotionally satisfying or more touching than many others, there is a commanding, magical, internal, musical tug-of-war going on here!

Ubi Caritas

Antiphon

U ~ bi cá~ ri ~ tas et am ~ or; De~us i~bi est.

Congre-gá~vit nos in u~num Christi am-or.

Ex-sul-té~mus, et in ip~so iu~cundé~mur.

Ti~me~á~mus et a~mé~mus De~um vi~vum.

Et ex corde di-li-gá~mus nos sin~cé~ro.

Antiphon.

A ~ men.

UBI CARITAS

In short, there are three things that last: faith, hope
and love; and the greatest of these is love.

1 Corinthians 13:13

ANTIPHON:

Ubi cáritas et amor,
Deus ibi est.

Congregávit nos in unum
Christi amor.

Exsultémus, et in ipso
jucundémur.

Timeámus et amémus Deum
vivum.

Et ex corde diligámus nos
sincéro.
ANTIPHON.

Simul ergo cum in únum
congregámur:

Ne nos ménte dividámur
caveámus.

Céssent jurgia malígna,
céssent lítes.

Et in médio nostri sit Chrístus
Deus.
ANTIPHON.

Simul quoque cum beátis
videámus.

Gloriánter vúltum túum,
Chríste Deus:

Gáudium quod est
imménsum , atque
próbum:

Saecúla per infiníta
saeculórum. Amen.

Where ever charity
and love flourish,
God is there. The love of
God has gathered us together,
let us rejoice, then and be
glad in Him. Let us fear and
love the living God. Let us
love one another from the
deepest parts of our hearts.
Therefore, when we are
together, let us be careful not
to be divided in mind. And
among us will be Christ our
God. And in company with
the blessed, may we see your
face in glory, Christ our God.
Pure and limitless joy, for
ever and ever. Amen.

MEDITATION

This song of justice and love was apparently written in Italy perhaps as early as the ninth century and it's as much a peace anthem for today's world of dissension and vacillation as it may have been then. I see it as a hugely important chant in these times of peacekeeping and peaceseeking, and I always integrate some phrases from it every time I walk through a group of people, singing to them.

Ne nos mente dividamur caveamus
(When we are together let us not be
divided in mind.)

Many issues of equality, justice and compassion hover around and through this chant. For instance, 'Ubi Caritas' is sung during the ritual of the washing of the feet on Maundy Thursday, the Thursday before Easter. This was the day when British kings traditionally gave specially minted coins to the poor.

For me all kinds of cultural barriers break down as this chant flies way up and beyond the belief system of the Roman Catholic Church. When I sing it I am always aware of the words of the greatest and most tireless fighter for human rights of our time, Mahatma Gandhi, who was himself strongly drawn to the theme of this anthem. In 1928 he wrote: 'Where love is, there is God also'. This remarkable Hindu pacifist achieved the status of Karma yogi during his lifetime. He himself describes the perfect yogi – which could as easily be the perfect Christian, or non-believer – as being 'a devotee who is jealous of none, who is a fount of mercy, who is selfless, who is ever forgiving, who has dedicated mind and soul to God'.

Mahatma Gandhi's life story is never far from my mind because of one enthralling biographical work which has influenced me over a long time. Most books come and go in our lives, often, as we say, 'going in one ear or eye and out the other'. But an abiding bookprint on me was the biography of Gandhi by journalist Louis Fischer.

I read it before I visited India for the first time in 1982, more out of a desire to tune in to the culture and the people than from an interest in Gandhi himself. Fischer, an American, paints a deeply moving picture of Gandhi's world, poetically amplifying the cultural and spiritual hybridisation between east and west. He relates that when Mahatma read the Beatitudes: 'Blessed are the poor in spirit ...' a recounting of the Sermon on the Mount in Matthew's Gospel, he wrote in his diaries that these golden laws 'went straight to my heart'. I was a slow starter on this saint, who died in 1948, but now he is firmly in my heart. Humour, lightheartedness and spirituality are always good combinations, and here's another Gandhian gem which makes me smile: 'But for my faith in God, I should have been a raving maniac!'

On a textual note to this chant, the antiphon runs in some sources as: *Ubi caritas est vera, Deus ibi est* (Where love is true, God is there). But we found this word-sequence a bit of a tongue-twister and we opted for the more mellifluent *Ubi caritas et amor.*

On a musical note, this chant seems to be crying out for another tune! The musical setting is spiky and uneasy, and the four-note antiphon *Ubi caritas et amor, Deus ibi est,* instead of flying up to the heavens along with the words, hangs in mid-air! So if you feel inspired to create another air, let me know!

I return to the east and to Gandhi to celebrate this song of Christian justice with a blessing, a blessing which unites us in the shared image of the Divine.

> God, as truth, has been for me
> a treasure beyond price,
> May he be so to every one of us.
>
> Mahatma Gandhi, 1935

Regnavit Dominus

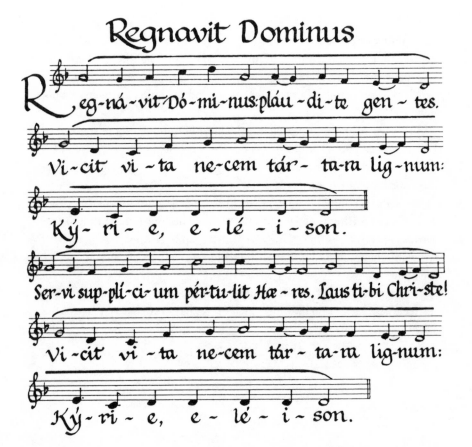

REGNAVIT DOMINUS

Clap your hands, all you peoples,
Acclaim God with shouts of joy;
Let the music sound for our God, let it sound.

Psalm 47:1, 6

Regnávit Dóminus:
pláudite gentes.
Vicit vita necem tártara
lignum:
Kyrie, eléison.

Servi supplícium pértulit
Haeres.
Laus tibi Christe!
Vicit vita necem tártara
lignum: Kyrie, eléison.

Fit nunc illé lapis, sprétus ab
hoste.
Jesus magna Deus questió
múndi: Kyrie, eléison.

Cur frendúnt populi! concidat
error!
Laus tibi Christe!
Jesus magna Deus questió
múndi:
Kyrie, eléison.

Qui pascís propria carne
redémptos,
Qui dítas roseo, sanguine labra:
Kyrie, eléison.

Praesta perpétuae gaudia
Paschae,
Laus tibi Christe!
Qui dítas roseo, sanguine
labra: Kyrie, eléison.

The Lord now reigns
ideed: clap your hands,
people. Life has defeated
death, wood the hellish
empire. Kyrie eleison. The
King himself has endured the
slave's torment. Praise to you,
Christ. The One rejected by
the enemy is now the central
one. Jesus, the great God, the
world's great talking point.
Kyrie eleison. Why do people
gnash their teeth! May
misguided thinking disappear!
Praise to you, Christ. You
who feed the redeemed with
your own body; who graces
our lips with your own red
blood. Kyrie eleison. Grant
us the joys of never-ending
Easter. Praise to you, Christ!

MEDITATION

Psalm 47, with its direct invitation to us to clap our hands, often springs to mind as I sing this chant. We are invited to do so in the first line *plaudite gentes* (clap your hands, people). The whole notion of clapping is thought-provoking – clapping as a measure of one's delight on receiving a gift perhaps, on hearing good news or even traumatic news. Claps which are not prolonged seem intuitive, instinctive. And what of the clapping at a performance? Speaking as a performer, the jarring sound of clapping after a song can interfere with that galaxy of sound and spirit which one has just painted. Genuine appreciation and sharing, I feel, is for the most part non-verbal, non-demonstrative – one can always sense the level of truth and integrity of any listening group. Of course, that is not to deny the huge thrill that a performer feels when the audience rises to applaud, to express enthusiastic approval. It is then that performer and audience must share the applause together because a performer cannot exist without an audience and no true audience exists without interaction with the performer. When Oscar Wilde was asked how the first performance of one of his plays went he replied: 'The play was a huge success. The audience, however, a complete failure!'

One beautiful mention of clapping comes from the First Book of Isaiah written in the eighth century BC. When you read it, let your soul go into that peace-filled world of fantasy, of imagination, of dreams:

> Yes, you will leave with joy,
> and be led away in peace.
> Mountains and hills will break forth before you singing
> and all the trees of the countryside clap their hands.
> Isaiah 55:12

Picturing and hearing the mountains, hills, all of nature clapping brings to mind the unique tradition of gestural approval which exists among the Samoan peoples. The inhabitants of the Pacific islands of Samoa, I believe, rub the palms of their hands together in a circular rhythmic motion, producing gestures and sounds which not only intensify one's own individual power but also enhance the cyclic energy between performer and listener. Try it for yourself. It's as if one is right there in the middle of a living rainforest, imitating the rustling wind and the falling raindrops.

'Regnavit Dominus' is an Easter chant from the Benedictine tradition of Monte Casino. It is a beautiful wedding of words and music, not really Gregorian Chant, but so what! For me there's a whole sense of pure joy in the final statement: *Laus tibi Christe* (Praise to you, Christ). The words of the chant seem to me a trifle doleful, but all is forgotten when this phrase appears. A useful chant for sharing because the second phrase with the little tail of *Kyrie eleison* keeps reappearing. For those who like to sing without having too much to learn it is ideal!

Near the cross of Jesus stood his mother.
John 19:25

Stabat Mater dolorósa
Juxta crucem lacrimósa,
Dum pendébat filius.

Cújus ánimam geméntem,
Contristátam et doléntem
Pertansívit gládius.

Eia Máter, fons amóris,
Me sentíre vim dolóris
Fac, ut técum lúgeam.

Fac ut árdea cor méum
In amándo Chrístum Deum,
Ut síbi compláceam.

Chríste, cum sit hinc exire,
Da per Mátrem me veníre
Ad pálmam victóriae.

Quando córpus moriétur,
Fac ut ánimae donétur
Paradísi glória. Amen.

The sorrowful mother was standing crying beside the Cross on which her son was hanging. Her soul was filled with grief, anguish and sorrow, because the sword of prophecy pierced it. Therefore, Mother, source of all love, make me understand the meaning of your sorrow that I may grieve with you. Make my heart burn with the love of Christ, my God, that he may look on me favourably. Christ, when it is time for me to leave this world, through your mother, give me the palm of victory. When my body is dead, grant that my soul be given the glory of Paradise. Amen.

MEDITATION

As I gather my thoughts for this amazing chant, my deepest feelings are heightened by the coincidence of this day being Good Friday. We do not know for certain who wrote this poignant lament and it has in various sources been ascribed to Saints Gregory, Bernard, Bonaventure, Jacopone da Todi, John XXII and Gregory XI. Whatever about authorship, tradition has it that 'Stabat Mater' was a processional chant. Hence, in reverence for and in memory of this tradition, I love to sing it in procession with others.

The sense of loss which this chant embodies and conveys came alive for me in a very real way in 1994 during three heart-rending journeys to war-torn Bosnia and Croatia. A small band of English people had visited some Christian and Muslim refugee camps, carrying food, clothing, and most of all offering their company and concern. As they left, they asked the inevitable question: 'What would you like us to bring back next time round?' The answer was unequivocal: music and song is what the refugees desired above all else.

Days later, I met these people in Holland for the first time, and months later I found myself in Croatia doing the grim rounds of camps. Through that chink in consciousness and memory brought to the surface by the 'Stabat Mater', I am now back there in a Muslim refugee camp in Samobor, Croatia. Landing down in grey, colourless Zagreb, the snows piled three inches high, one immediately felt that even the elements were angry at the overt manifestation of 'man's inhumanity to man'. Next evening I was to sing at a Muslim camp aptly called 'The Barracks'. Over two hundred people lived there temporarily, strangers to one another mostly, united only in their shared belief in another world above and beyond their hell of reality. The Barracks was just a series of temporary wooden huts, the walls seeping and the floors soggy with dampness.

About seventy people – men, scarfed women and wide-eyed, frightened children – crowded into a dimly-lit room in one of these huts. Some sat on the few chairs scattered around, some huddled on the humid ground, while the men stood sheepishly at the back. Through the unreality of my own presence there, I had to smile as I beheld the physical hierarchy of men, women and children. It brought back images of Sunday Mass in rural Ireland where the men also huddle at the back of the church! The interpreter who was to present my songs failed to show up because of the snow, so after fifteen minutes of gazing and smiling at one another, I intuitively knew the right moment to break the silence.

The performance dynamic was extraordinary. A nervous, uneasy smile broke over people's faces, children nudged one another timidly, and then there was a split-second transformation and we were all caught up in something happening. Those people froze, ghostlike, following my every step and note as I walked the human labyrinth there, matching it with a maze of improvisatory, spur-of-the-moment songs, anything that came into my head. I became the song in a way which has never happened to me before or since that evening. Time stopped still for over an hour, I believe. Songs from the Irish tradition, indeed some songs from early childhood which I never really knew I had, spiritual songs from many traditions, visionary chants, Gregorian Chants, chants of the German medieval mystic Hildegard Von Bingen, all chose their moment.

Two songs kept revisiting my mind, wanting to be sung and resung, again and again: a pre-Christian lament (a *caoineadh*) from Donegal, the pathetic, distraught cry of a mother who has lost her baby, never to see or touch her again; the second song to demand attention over and over was the great 'Stabat Mater', the song of despair, of terrible bereavement. It was the last song I sang for the inmates of The Barracks.

Three months later, again on the same mission, which this time took in Sarajevo to plant a peace flame on the bridge there, I enquired about the fate of The Barracks. 'Strange that you should ask,' was the reply, 'because last night The Barracks was evacuated.' In the middle of the night the Muslims had all been moved to other front-line camps, once more torn apart and in havoc. Together with a small group of people and two other artists – a dancer and a mime artist – I made a pilgrimage that afternoon to the harrowing shell of The Barracks. As we picked our steps through the chaos, I could almost hear the cries of horror, just a few hours earlier, as men, women and children grasped what they could, groping in the dark to hold on to anything at all in their nightmare of survival.

Then, amidst mounds of discarded clothes and shoes, babies' bottles and toys, Roy, the dancer among us, moved with the same ghostlike timelessness of my earlier memory; Jonathan, the mime artist, simulated the hopelessness of it all, slowly picking a rag-doll from the rubble, then gazing wistfully out the paneless window, first in the direction of the far-off hills which now cradled the former inhabitants, and then towards the skies which expressed the ultimate hopelessness – and hope – of it all. All I could do was sing the 'Stabat Mater' through the truest crevice of my soul, at first in a strangulated, insecure voice of despair, but gradually, as gratitude for this experience, for song and sharing, grew, I found myself singing the notes nearest to God which I would ever reach.

This fourteenth-century song of death and destruction will never be the same for me again. It symbolises a spontaneous ritual of spiritual cleansing, a purifying anthem of and for the cosmos! It will always bring with it memories not just of The Barracks, but of people everywhere who are thrust into the depths of despair. Children lost, homeless, trying to fend for themselves; mothers lamenting children – living hell on earth. But even more importantly, the 'Stabat Mater' embodies the physical processing so essential to survival, that life-giving moving of the spirit that springs into being when all is lost and one is powerless; to sing and to process during that singing – sometimes this is all we have.

> The first Day's night had come –
> And grateful that a thing
> So terrible – had been endured –
> I told my Soul to sing –
>
> Emily Dickinson

Grief and loss are universal, but within the story of Ireland's traditional spirituality there are very significant similarities of expression. Visualising Mary at the foot of the cross in the 'Stabat Mater', lamenting or keening her son, the whole genre of song from the Irish tradition called 'Caoineadh na dTrí Muire' (The Lament of the Three Marys) floods into the imagination. In these songs the intensity of the experience of loss and suffering comes alive and personal through the direct dialogue between Mary and Jesus. A translation of just eight of the two-lined stanzas from the Irish gives the flavour of a spirituality renowned for its intimacy. The poetic translation below, which I love to quote and ponder on, was created by the Irish poet Gabriel Rosenstock some years ago for my first-ever recording of religious song.

> Peter, apostle, have you seen my love so bright?
> M'ochón 's m'ochón ó!
> I saw him midst his enemies, a harrowing sight.
> M'ochón 's m'ochón ó!
> Who is that fine man on the Passion Tree?

M'ochón 's m'ochón ó!
'Tis your son, dear mother, know you not me?
M'ochón 's m'ochón ó!
Is that the wee babe I bore nine months in my womb?
M'ochón 's m'ochón ó!
That was born in a stable when no house would give us room,
M'ochón 's m'ochón ó!
Mother be quiet, let not your heart be torn,
M'ochón 's m'ochón ó!
My keening women are yet to be born,
M'ochón 's m'ochón ó!

Gabriel Rosenstock

Here reason and raging are carefully and pathetically balanced between the rational conversation of Mary, Peter and Jesus on the one hand, and the tearful cries of grief, *ochón* (a traditional keening or mourning word), on the other. This heart-rending sigh of lament is even further heightened as Mary makes it her own by personifying it when she says, *m'ochón agus m'ochón ó!* (*my* sorrow and my pain).

But tears are part of loss in all its many forms – physical loss, loss in relationship, even the natural loss-pangs of seeing your child go to school on that first day. In four short lines Emily Dickinson sums it up!

It's such a little thing to weep –
So short a thing to sigh –
And yet – by Trades – the size of these
We men and women die!

The last word on this Good Friday canticle I leave to the great English contemporary poet Geoffrey Hill, whose 'Canticle for Good Friday' traces that last horrific Cross crucible, the ultimate crucible of Christ:

The cross staggered him. At the cliff-top
Thomas, beneath its burden, stood
While the dulled wood
Spat on the stones each drop
Of deliberate blood.

A clamping, cold-figured day
Thomas (not transfigured) stamped, crouched,
Watched

Smelt vinegar and blood. He,
As yet unsearched, unscratched,

And suffered to remain
At such near distance
(A slight miracle might cleanse
His brain
Of all attachments, claw-roots of sense)

In unaccountable darkness moved away,
The strange flesh untouched, carrion-sustenance
Of staunchest love, choicest defiance,
Creation's issue congealing (and one woman's).

Geoffrey Hill

Pange Lingua

an-ge lin-gua, glo - ri - ó - si

Cór - po - ris my- sté - ri - um

San-gui- nís-que pre - ti - ó - si

quem in mun-di pré - ti - um

Fruc-tus ven-tris ge — ne - ró - si

Rex ef-fú-dit gén - ti- um. A ~ men.

PANGE LINGUA

Esther's reply:
Go and assemble and fast for me. Do not eat or drink
for three days. For my part, I and my maids
will keep the same fast.

Esther 4:16

Pange lingua, gloriósi
Córporis mystérium
Sanguinísque pretiósi
Quem in mundi pretium
Fructus ventris generósi
Rex effúdit géntium.

Tantum ergo Sacraméntum
Venerémur cérnui:
Et antíquum documéntum
Nóvo cédat rítui:
Praéstet fídes suppleméntum
Sénsuum deféctui.

Genitóri, Genitóque
Laus et jubilátio,
Salus, honor, virtus quoque
Sit et benedíctio:
Procedénti ab utróque
Cómpar sit laudátio. Amen.

Sing, my tongue, and praise the mystery of the glorious body and the most precious blood. Which was shed to save the world by the King of the people, the fruit of a venerable womb. Therefore, let us bow and worship in the light of so great a mystery; let the laws of the ancient rite give way to the new gospel rite. Let faith help and support us to make up for the inadequacies of our senses. Let us praise and joyfully sing to the Father and the Son, who is saving power, honour, might and every blessing; and to the Spirit who proceeds from both in glory. Amen

VICTIMAE PASCHALI

Jesus said to her, 'Do not cling to me ...
I am ascending to my Father and your Father,
to my God and your God.'
So Mary of Magdala went and told the disciples that
she had seen the Lord and that he had said
these things to her.

John 20:17-18

Víctimae Pascháli
laudes, immolent
Christiáni,
Agnus redémit oves:
Christus ínnocens Patri
reconciliávit peccatóres.
Mors et vita duéllo conflixére
mirándo, dux vitae
mórtuus, regnat vivus.
'Dic nobis María, quid vidísti
in via!'
'Sepúlchrum Christi vivéntis,
et glóriam vidi resurgéntis:
Angelicos testes sudárium et
vestes.
Surréxit Christus spes mea
praecédet suos in
Galilaéam.'
Credéndum est magi soli,
Maríae veráci, quam
judaeorum turbae falláci.
Scimus Christum surrexísse a
mórtuis vere, tu nobis,
victor Rex, miserére.

Let Christians offer their
sacrifice of praise to the
Paschal Victim. A lamb
redeems the sheep: the
innocent Christ has reconciled
sinners to the Father. Death
and life have fought duel with
one another in an amazing
battle, the leader of life who
was dead, lives and reigns.
'Tell us, Mary, what did you
see on the way!' I saw the
tomb of the living Christ, and
the glory of the resurrection:
Angelic witnesses, the cloth
and the shroud. Christ my
hope has risen, he goes before
his own into Galilee. The true
Mary alone is to be believed
rather than the lying jews. We
know that Christ has truly
risen from the dead, you,
Victor King, have mercy on us.

Victimæ Paschali

Víctimæ Pascháli laudes ím-mo-lent Chri-sti-á-ni,

Ag-nus re-dé-mit o-ves:Chri-stus ín-no-cens Pa-tri

re-con-ci- li- á-vit pec-ca- tó- res.

Mors et vi-ta du-él-lo con-fli-xé-re mi-rán-do,

dux vi- tæ mór-tu- us, reg-nat vi- vus.

Dic no-bis, Ma-rí- a, quid vi-dí-sti in vi-a?

Se - púl-chrum Chri-sti vi- vén- tis, et

gló- ri- am vi-di re- sur-gén- tis.

An-gé-li- cos tes-tes su-dá-ri- um et ves-tes.

Sur-réx- it Chri-stus spes me — a, præ-

cé-det su-os in Ga-li-læ — am.

Cre-dén-dum est ma-gi so-li, Ma-rí-æ ve-rá-ci,

quam Ju- dæ-ó-rum tur-bæ fal-lá-ci.

Sci-mus Chri-stum surrex-is-se a mórtu-is ve-re,

tu no-bis, vic-tor Rex, mi-se-ré — re.

MEDITATION

The midnight – when noon is born

Chinese proverb

From the 'unaccountable darkness' of history and of the here-and-now, we sing our way to Resurrection through two Easter chants from the Middle Ages, 'Pange Lingua' and 'Victimae Paschali Laudes'. Winter solstice gives way to the vernal equinox as we toast the goddess Éostre, whose feast was celebrated at this time. It was the Venerable Bede, a seventh-century English Benedictine, who wedded the Christian and pre-Christian by naming the festival commemorating the resurrection of Christ after this goddess. These two historical chant classics mark that period of suspense – the space between darkness and light, between unknowing and knowing – which is the very essence of this time of year as it manifests itself nature-wise in spring.

Spring is the Period
Express from God.
Among the other seasons
Himself abide,

But during March and April
None stir abroad
Without a cordial interview
With God.

Emily Dickinson

There is a superabundance of greening, blossoming apple trees, of lambing, hatching, new life everywhere. For our foreparents before us tending one's physical patch went hand-in-hand with tending the spiritual as Good Friday was traditionally a day for weeding both the garden of the soil and the garden of the soul!

'Pange Lingua' carries me back in time to thirty-two years ago! I had just begun an educational pilgrimage of five years at St Louis convent, Dundalk, County Louth, in the north-east of Ireland. Gratitude and blessedness sum up that time for introducing me to the world of Gregorian Chant and the honeyed sounds of Latin. There, on Sundays, at the sometimes dreaded Holy Hour, we 'religiously' sang our hearts out through 'Pange Lingua' in the very form that I sing it for you now – one verse of 'Pange Lingua' and the two-verse 'Tantum Ergo'. Having little feeling for this exquisite little work of art at the time, what kept us going sometimes was the unspoken promise of apple tart and custard which was the customary dessert for Sunday lunch!

Composed by the Dominican theologian Thomas Aquinas in 1264, the hymn was commissioned by Pope Urban IV at the establishment of a new feast – Corpus Christi – honouring the body of Christ. The majesty and sublimity of this chant lies in its classical construction of three sets of two lines, mirroring each other with eight syllables in the first and seven in the second, and all three sets following the same rhyming pattern. This very strict word-structure is contrasted with the music, where caution is thrown to the wind and the music is new and fresh for each of the six lines. Ingenious!

'Victimae Paschali' is another historical chant which flows with similar momentum and direction. It is a marvellous re-enactment of the day of the resurrection of Christ – the day of resurrection of us all! Somehow or other the opposite poles of life and death, from the womb to the tomb, are explored, meditated upon and resolved within a mini-drama which is over nine hundred years old! This Easter Sequence – a form of religious poetry of the Middle Ages sung during Mass after the Gradual and Alleluia – is ascribed to Wipo, a Burgundian priest who was chaplain to King Conrad II and tutor of Henry III. He died around the year of 1050. A melodrama, this piece is described in the *Antiphonale Sarisburiense*, a very important collection of British Gregorian Chant from the cathedral church of Salisbury (*c.*1360). We have our own Irish version in the beautiful fourteenth-century manuscript from Marsh's Library in Dublin. Last week, under the guidance of this library's guardian angel, Muriel McCarthy, I, almost not believing what I was holding in my hands, carefully and reverently handled every awe-inspiring page of this manuscript. What a privilege!

'Victimae Paschali', along with its visual illumination through the manuscript and its recreation in sound, spirit and drama, represents the entire gamut of dialogue and exchange between art, spirituality and aesthetics. Surely no more powerful and definitive proof of the existence of artistic interconnectedness and cross-fertilisation! Just one other specific detail on our rendering here. In a revision of the text in 1570, the Roman missal omits the verse 'Credendum'. The story goes that this was intended as a gesture towards the Jews but this, the textbooks tell us, is unlikely because the omission was made during the reign of Pius IV who was noted for his maltreatment of Jews, expelling them from Papal states and treating those who remained on humiliating terms. So, another mystery! We've restored this verse here in an open spirit of reverence for history, art, music and you, the understanding listener!

O FILII ET FILIAE

Yahweh my Lord is my strength,
he makes my feet as light as a doe's,
he makes me walk on the heights.

Habakkuk 3:19

O Filii et Filiæ

Alleluia, alle-lú-ia, alle-lú-ia.

O fi-li-i et fi-li-æ,

Rex cæ-lés-tis, Rex gló-ri-æ

Morte surréx-it hó-di-e, alle-lú-ia.

ANTIPHON:

Allelúia, allelúia, allelúia.

O fílii et filiae, Rex
caelestis, Rex gloriae
Morte surrexit hodie,
Allelúia. ANTIPHON.

Et máne príma sábbati,
Ad óstium monuménti
Accessérunt discípuli.
Allelúia. ANTIPHON.

Et María Magdaléne,
Et Jacóbi, et Salóme,
Venérunt córpus úngere.
Allelúia. ANTIPHON.

Béati qui non vidérunt,
Et fírmiter credidérunt,
Vitam aetérnam habébunt.
Allelúia. ANTIPHON.

Ex quíbus nos humílimas
Devótas atque débitas,
Déo dicámus Grátias.
Allelúia. ANTIPHON.

O sons and daughters,
the King of Heaven,
the King of Glory has risen
from the dead today. At first
light on Sunday, the disciples
made their way to the tomb.
And Mary Magdalen, Mary,
the mother of James and
Mary Salome came to prepare
the body with oils. Blessed
are those who have not seen
and firmly believe. They shall
have eternal life. For all these
things, let us, humbly,
devoutly and gratefully, give
thanks to God.

MEDITATION

Our seventh Easter poem was probably composed by French Franciscan Jean Tisserand (d. 1494). It first appeared in a booklet published in France in the mid-sixteenth century, where it consists of nine stanzas. Three more were added later. It is a great processional hymn, and true to tradition a few years ago a large gathering of us processed onto a beach in County Louth, singing this to the skies. It was early morning and we beheld the rising sun there. Then we walked home again, weary, exhilarated – all the time singing this chant trilingually in Latin, English and Irish, until we were almost entranced!

I have no idea who did the homely, uncluttered Irish version of 'O Filii', but I do know where I heard it first. It was in An Rinn Gaeltacht, then an Irish-speaking district in County Waterford, where we spent the early days of our married lives encountering for the first time our own naïve wildness and the wildness of the nearby, visible, Atlantic sea! I enclose two verses here, the second verse has that characteristic An Rinn pronunciation of the word *Tá*, which sounds 'Haw' instead of the more usual 'Thaw'. To sing anything other than this would be a sacrilege!

> A phobail Dé, a mhuintir ghroí,
> Le háthas is le lúcháir croí,
> Fáiltímís don aiséirí, Alleluia!

> Thá áthas ar fud an domhain mhór,
> Ón uair gur eirig ár Slánaitheoir,
> Mac Muire Naofa, 'Sé Dia na nGlóir, Alleluia!

My favourite Latin verse runs: *Beati qui viderunt* ... 'Blessed are those who have not seen and firmly believe, they will have eternal life.' Oh! to possess such faith and confidence, but then even a saint didn't have it. The story goes that St Catherine of Siena, the fourteenth-century mystic, political and social activist (although she never learned to write) once nagged and accused the Lord for not being there with her in her trials and temptations. But the Lord replied: 'I was in your heart all the time, Catherine, because I will not leave anyone who does not leave me first.'

This little legend is just another version of what is found in *Footsteps*, which I carry constantly in my purse. Many of you will know it, so I'll trim it down a trifle.

As Everyman and his maker look back over the sands of creation, their two sets of footsteps are clearly visible as they walk hand in hand. But at many stages along the pilgrimage, only two footprints appear.
'Why did you abandon me, then?' asks Everyman.
'I never abandoned you,' said the Creator. 'That was when I carried you on my back!'

Above all else, 'O Filii' is a real social chant, waiting to be sung with great gusto and fervour, and it is easy to see why, when you match the visual with the aural. It's strange what happens when you translate a sound which lives only in the ear of the mind to a medium which becomes a sound for the eye! Most times it frees the senses to interact and bond in a masterly blend of harmonic sound and sight. Sometimes, however, it freezes these same senses and hinders one's sense of the sense of it all! 'O Filii' is the near-perfect example of the freeing experience and just by looking at the notes in the above transcription, you'll see what I mean. I'll talk you through a little, just in case, because this is surely nerve-centre stuff!

Immediately, the setting of the three Alleluias is totally absorbing – five notes to sing out the first two, four to sing the third. Then the verse takes over. Ten notes for the first phrase, the same ten notes again for the second phrase, and lo and behold, the same ten notes of the first two Alleluias for the next line of text – and the chant ends on the high notes of the final Alleluia. Perfect balance, based not on mundane patterns but on unpredictability.

Just talking about the air has me right back binding musical air here with misty elemental air in the church of the Benedictine community of Glenstal Abbey. Words can never physically recreate any fragrance, not to speak of the aroma of the pungent incense during the final procession in the abbey at what, for me, is the most moving and moody ceremony within the entire Church cycle of seasons – that after the Easter midnight vigil.

This was the final chant of our recording session and as I replay it now, I find it has all of that distinctive 'one for the road' feel about it! We were dizzy with the twirling of this cyclical Alleluia music, going round and round, forming a busy circle of life and prayer. We were subconsciously tuning in to the very universe from where we sang, and the Holy Spirit whom we honour next was our trusty axis!

THE
GOLDEN
SEQUENCE

Pentecost comes from a Greek word *Pentékosté* which means 'fifty', and so this Christian feast is celebrated just fifty days after Easter – the seventh Sunday after. Long ago, we used to call this day Whit Sunday, after an ancient custom of the newly-baptised dressing in white on this day. Celebrating the advent of the Holy Spirit to us all, we want to sing for you this exhilarating whitsong.

VENI, SANCTE SPIRITUS

The Holy Spirit makes a soul whole and strong
in the right faith and the right belief.

Julian of Norwich (1343-1413)

Veni, Sancte Spíritus,
Et emítte caélitus,
Lucis tuae rádium.
Veni, pater páuperum,
Veni dator múnerum,
Veni lumen córdium.
Consolátor óptime,
Dulcis hospes ánimae,
Dulce refrigérium.
In labóre requies,
In aestu tempéries,
In fletu solátium.
O lux beatíssima,
Reple cordis íntima,
Tuórum fidélium.
Sine tuo númine
Nihil est in hómine,
Nihil est innóxium.
Lava quod est sórdidum,
Riga quod est áridum,
Sana quod est sáucium.
Flecte quod est rígidum,
Fove quod est frígidum,
Rege quod est dévium.
Da tuis fidélibus,
In te confidéntibus,
Sacrum septenárium.
Da virtútis méritum,
Da salútis éxitum,
Da perénne gáudium.

Come, Holy Spirit, and from heaven pour forth the rays of your light. Come, father of the poor, come, giver of gifts, come light of hearts. Best of consolers, sweet dweller of the soul, sweet consolation. Rest in labour, coolness in heat, comfort in distress. O most blessed light fill the most intimate hearts of your faithful ones. Without your presence, man is nothing, nothing is sinless. Cleanse what is sordid, moisturise what is dry, heal what is wounded. Make flexible what is inflexible, warm what is frigid, straighten what is crooked. In you we trust. Give your faithful your seven gifts. Give them merit for their virtuous deeds, give them a safe salvation, give them neverending happiness.

Veni, Sancte Spiritus

e-ni, Sancte Spí ~ ri-tus, Et e ~ mít-te
2. Ve-ni, pa-ter páu-pe-rum, Ve-ni da-tor

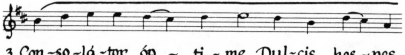

cœ ~ li ~ tus Lu-cis tu-œ rá ~ di-um.
mú ~ ne-rum, Ve-ni, lu-men cór ~ di-um.

3. Con-so-lá-tor óp ~ ti-me, Dul-cis hos-pes
4. In la-bó-re re ~ qui ~ es, In œ-stu tem-

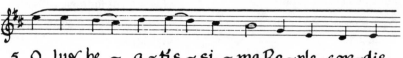

á ~ ni-mœ, Dul-ce re ~ fri-gé ~ ri-um.
pé ~ ri ~ es, Infle-tu so ~ lá ~ ti-um.

5. O lux be ~ a-tís-si-ma, Re-ple cor-dis
6. Si-ne tu- o nú-mi-ne Ni-hil est in

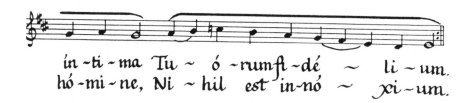

ín ~ti ~ ma Tu ~ ó ~rumfl ~dé ~ li ~ um.
hó ~mi ~ ne, Ni ~ hil est in ~ nó ~ xi ~ um.

7. La ~ va quod est sór ~ di ~dum, Ri ~ga quod
8. Flec ~ te quod est rí ~ gi ~dum, Fo ~ ve quod

est á ~ ri ~dum, Sa ~na quod est sáu ~ci ~ um.
est frí ~ gi ~dum, Re ~ ge quod est dé ~vi ~ um.

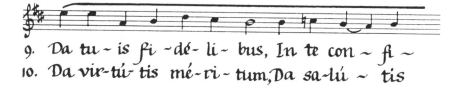

9. Da tu ~ is fi ~dé ~ li ~ bus, In te con ~ fi ~
10. Da vir ~ tú ~ tis mé ~ ri ~ tum, Da sa ~ lú ~ tis

dén ~ ti ~ bus, Sa ~ crum sep ~ te ~ ná ~ ri ~ um.
éx ~ i ~ tum, Da per ~ én ~ ne gáu ~ di ~ um.

MEDITATION

'Veni Sancte Spiritus' has been sung repeatedly throughout the ages on all occasions when the people of God need the grace of the Holy Spirit. For me it holds a particular memory. In 1991, our eldest son, Eoin, was confirmed in the parish of Murroe, County Limerick, on the eve of Pentecost. At 5pm that Saturday evening I was to begin the long, tedious pilgrimage to Brazil to sing at a United Nations Conference in Rio de Janeiro. Because of staying for the confirmation, a very tight schedule had been planned for me, so in less than two hours after I had touched down in Rio, I was due to sing at the final session of the World Spiritual and Religious Leaders assembly. With 'Veni Sancte Spiritus' singing in my soul, off I went.

After some twenty-two hours above the clouds, I arrived in Brazil at midday on Pentecost Sunday. However, my instruments and belongings had not arrived – and had been sent instead to the Philippines when we'd stopped over in Miami! And here I was in jeans and tee-shirt due to sing in two hours' time! A friend came to the rescue with a long, flowing mauve gown. I closed my eyes and sang this chant from the deepest place inside me to the closing session there.

Stephen Langton (c. 1150-1228), who was Archbishop of Canterbury, is probably the author of 'Veni Sancte Spiritus'. It is a chant of justice, peace and healing, and stands as a lighthouse on the shores of universal spirituality and morality. It is a Whitsun sequence referred to as 'The Golden Sequence'.

I always feel that it's a moody chant to sing and listen to. Although seemingly simply created, like all timeless works of art it is extremely carefully, thoughtfully and sensitively designed, each jigsaw piece falling easily and obviously into place before our eyes.

Here are just some of its treasures. Three short phrases go to make up an entity or full phrase. Then the music comes back again with a new set of verbal clothes. To indicate this musical return in the transcription I've used the most frequently employed traditional method, that of a symbol of two dots centring on the second and third spaces – like little dark eyes looking back over, guiding and blessing every note!

Each short phrase is built with seven syllabic bricks (the number seven cleverly chosen, no doubt, because it is the seventh Sunday celebration). This gives us twenty-one syllables in all – three sets of seven in every verse. Then, for further synchronicity and structural ingenuity, syllables seven and fourteen are identical in every verse. But the pure poetry of it all reaches its own seventh heaven by ending every single verse on *ium*! No surprise that it became known as 'The Golden Sequence'.

To capture the mood of this amazing, spirit-filled chant, I chose the words in the quotation above of English mystic and recluse Julian of Norwich, from a fascinating dialogue between her and another contemporary visionary, Margery Kempe. When Margery, guided by the Holy Spirit, renounced her marriage, she was called by God to go to Julian for counsel. In the words above, Julian confirms and comforts her, assuring her of the presence of the Holy Spirit in her soul. However, it appears from Margery's spellbinding autobiography – the first-ever autobiography in English, but written in the removed third person – that she had a particularly difficult time following this indwelling of the Holy Spirit and at times seems possessed and irrational, fleeing from reality.

Five hundred years later Emily Dickinson was also obsessed with things of the spirit, and with this duality of fleeing from but being drawn inexorably towards reality. A wonderful poem of hers uncannily describes that sense of not feeling at home on earth, a feeling which comes to all of us at one stage or another. Then the frantic thought flows out: maybe I won't feel at home in heaven either!

> I never felt at Home – Below –
> And in the Handsome Skies
> I shall not feel at Home – I know –
> I don't like Paradise –
> Because it's Sunday – all the time –
> And Recess – never comes –
> And Eden'll be so lonesome
> Bright Wednesday Afternoons –
> If God could make a visit –
> Or ever took a Nap –
> So not to see us – but they say
> Himself – a Telescope
> Perennial beholds us –
> Myself would run away
> From Him – and Holy Ghost – and All –
> But there's the 'Judgment Day'!
>
> Emily Dickinson

THE
ETERNAL WHEELS

CHRISTUS

Verbum caro factum est, alle-lú-ia, al-le- lu- ia.

℣. Et ha-bi-tá-vit in no-bis. ℟. Al-le- lú-ia, al-le-lú- ia.

℣. Gló-ri-a Pa-tri et Fí-li- o et Spi-rí-tu-i Sanc-to.
D.C. al Fine.

VERBUM CARO FACTUM EST

The word of God is something alive and active:
it cuts like any double-edged sword but more finely:
it can slip through the place where the soul is
divided from the spirit, or joints from the marrow;
it can judge the secret emotions and thoughts.

Hebrews. 4:12-13

Verbum caro factum est,
Allelúia, allelúia.
Et habitávit in nobis.
Allelúia, alleluia.
Glória Patri et Fílio et
Spíritui Sancto.
Verbum caro factum est,
Allelúia, allelúia.

The Word was made
flesh, Alleluia, alleluia.
And dwelt amongst us.
Alleluia, alleluia. Glory be to
the Father, and to the Son,
and to the Holy Spirit. The
Word was made flesh,
Alleluia, alleluia.

MEDITATION

The Prologue from St John's Gospel is the source of this text:

> The Word was made flesh,
> he lived among us,
> and we saw his glory,
> the glory that is his as the only Son of the Father,
> full of grace and truth.
>
> John 1:14

Inspiring words. Throw in on top of that six Alleluias and it's a prayer!

'Verbum Caro' was the very last solo which I recorded and it just slipped in the back door! I had been singing 'Pange Lingua' for you and as I waited for the technical side of the recording to be put in place, I just noticed this chant which I had never paid any attention to before. In one take, it immediately came alive off the page. So I baptise this chant in your presence and it is now firmly in my heart for ever more!

Jesu, Dulcis Memoria

Jesu, dulcis memória, Dans vera cordis gáudia: sed super mel et ómnia Ejus dulcis præséntia.

A-men.

JESU, DULCIS MEMORIA

Sing to Yahweh, all the earth.
Proclaim his salvation day after day,
tell of his glory among the nations,
tell his marvels to every people.

Song of David, Chronicles 16:23-24

Jesu, dulcis memória,
Dans vera cordis gáudia;
sed super mel et ómnia,
Ejus dulcis praeséntia.

Nil cánitur suávius,
Nil audítur jucúndius,
Nil cogitátur dúlcius,
Quam Jesus Dei Fílius.

Sis Jesu nostrum gáudium,
Qui es futúrus praémium.
Sit nostra in te glória,
Per cuncta semper saécula.

Jam prosequamur laudibus,
Hymnís Jesum et précibus:
Ut nos donet caélestibus,
Cum ipso fruí sedibus.
Amen.

Jesus, sweet memory giving pure joys to the heart, but his presence is sweeter than honey and everything else besides. Nothing sweeter is sung, nothing more pleasing is heard, nothing to equal the thought of Jesus, the son of God. May Jesus be our reward in the future, may our glory be in you, for ever and ever. Let us follow Jesus with praises, hymns and prayers, that he may invite us to share heaven with him. Amen.

O LUX BEATA TRINITAS

You are Three and One.

St Francis of Assisi (1181-1226)

O lux beáta Trínitas,
   Et principális Unitas:
Jam sol recédit ígneus,
Infunde lumen córdibus.

Te mane laudum cármine
Te deprecémur véspere
Te nostra supplex glória
Per cuncta laudet sáecula.

Deo Patri sit glória
Ejúsque soli Fílio
Cum Spíritu Paráclito
Et nunc et in perpétuum.
   Amen.

O Blessed Light of the Trinity, the fiery sun is already receding. To you this morning we made humble prayer when we sang your praise and we do so now at evening. Grant to us that we may praise you forever. Glory to God the Father and to his only Son with the Holy Spirit both now and forever.

TE LUCIS ANTE TERMINUM

Never let the sun set on your anger
or else you will give the devil a foothold.

Ephesians 4:27

Te lucis ante términum,
Rerum Creátor póscimus,
Ut sólita cleméntía
Sis praesul ad custódiam.

Procul recédant sómnia,
Et nóctium phantásmata:
Hostémque nostrum cómprime,
Ne polluántur córpora.

Praesta, Pater omnípotens,
per Jesum Christum Dóminum,
qui tecum in perpétuum
regnat cum Sancto Spíritu.
    Amen.

Before the day is finished,
Creator of the world, we
earnestly ask you that
according to your mercy, you
be our protector and defence.
May no bad dreams, no
nightly fears come near us.
Protect us from our enemy so
that our bodies will not be
tainted. Almighty Father,
keep us, through Jesus Christ,
the Lord, who reigns with
you for ever with the Holy
Spirit. Amen.

MEDITATION

It seemed right to sing and keep these three little gems together. Here's a test for you now: take the first verse of each of these three jaunty hymns. On the side of your cheek, mark the syllables of each line with your fingers. How many do you get in each line of 'Jesu Dulcis Memoria'? How many in 'O Lux'? How many in 'Te Lucis'? Yes, each and every line of the three hymns has *eight* syllables each!

St Ambrose, founder of Western hymnody, created this simple mould or structure of what's called iambic dimeters. This hymn pattern was to prove extremely popular and remained a bestseller for nearly twelve hundred years.

Now, how does the music match or heighten the words? Well, 'Te Lucis Ante Terminum' has one note per syllable systematically throughout. 'O Lux Beata Trinitas', ascribed to St Ambrose himself, has random two-note syllables dotted throughout. But 'Jesu Dulcis Memoria' takes the biscuit! It has one note for each syllable until the end of the third line when, almost as if wanting us to realise that we're on the third line, the poet puts three notes on the last syllable. St Bernard of Clairvaux, patron of beekeepers and candlemakers, is very often credited as poet of 'Jesu Dulcis Memoria', this sparkling hymn to the Holy Name. However, it seems more likely that it was penned by some unknown English Cistercian of the thirteenth century. (Incidentally, there are forty-two verses altogether, but we decided at the last minute to sing only four!)

The two hymns 'Te Lucis Ante Terminum' and 'O Lux Beata Trinitas' make a fine pair! First of all, they are evening prayers which nobly turn us to face the setting sun in quiet and humble praise. Communal evening gatherings of Vespers and, later, Compline provide the backdrop for the airing of these hymns – 'O Lux Beata' at Sunday Vespers and 'Te Lucis' at Compline.

Vespers hymns generally wear two seasonal musical hats, having one melody for winter and one for summer. I chose the summer version of 'Te Lucis' because it is brimful of light, warmth, sunshine, and when I sing it I can hear the buzzing of the bees all around me!

Now, before you give 'O Lux' a go yourself let me say that it's a strange little hymn to sing. It almost runs away with you, tripping lightly over the notes in a frenzy of Trinitarian praise. As I sing it, the image of a constantly flowing circle of sound is in my head and I love to follow my own notes with the identical notes on the surpeti – a cat-and-mouse (and bee) chase! Of the dozen hymns ascribed directly to Ambrose, this one is my true delight!

> *Te lucis ante*, so devoutly he
> Breathed forth, so sweet the singing syllables,
> All sense of self was ravished out of me.
> The others joined their sweet, devout appeals
> To his, and sang the whole hymn afterward,
> Fixing their eyes on the eternal wheels.
>
> Dante Alighieri

So wrote the towering figure of medieval Italy, Dante Alighieri (1265-1321) in the great Christian epic *The Divine Comedy*. 'Te Lucis Ante Terminum' was sung so sweetly in purgatory, he says, that it transported him above and beyond. This is 'music that you would never have known to listen for' as Seamus Heaney says wistfully – uncannily perfect words to describe this air – an air which was in the air for at least six hundred years before Dante was born!

Nothing I say could enhance the delicate thread of the melody here, it is so perfect. It spans just six notes, and singing it is like balancing on a wheel of fortune! You never know what note you're going to land on!

This is a hymn for protection through the darkness, the night, and then in the move out into the light again through fears and nightmares. So it is appropriate that during Dante's journeying with Virgil through hell and purgatory he should hear, listen and be moved and healed at eventide by the eight-a-line 'singing syllables' of 'Te Lucis Ante Terminum'.

I love to rattle this out at Compline in Glenstal Abbey where, every second week, the melody carries the following words in English – you may wish to rattle it off yourself this evening about 8.45pm, and I'm sure we'll all be together somewhere in spirit and prayer!

> True Light, of God the Father born,
> The joy of man whom God has blessed,
> O Christ as Lord of night and day,
> The darkness of this world dispel.
>
> We pray to you, our loving Lord,
> To keep us through these coming hours:
> In you may our true rest be found
> As we entrust ourselves to sleep.

Keep far from us all taint of sin,
Our hearts set firm on you their God,
Watch over with your tender care
The servants purchased by your blood.

To you, O Christ, we make this prayer,
Through you, we sing the Father's praise,
One in the Spirit given us,
When you were lifted up on high.

If these night prayers prove too lofty for you and you are in the mood for something simpler, let Dag Hammarskjöld, Scandinavian philosopher, poet, first Secretary-general of the United Nations, say goodnight for you:

Night is drawing nigh –
For all that has been – Thanks!
For all that shall be – Yes!

There are cartloads of poems and prayers communicating the uneasy feelings of insomnia which we all experience at some time. Tossing and turning in bed at night, maybe waking early, troubled when fears seem insurmountable. I often wonder if this kind of blackness is physical. Perhaps the psyche's blood flow is affected when one lies flat?

At any rate, the cloud lifts considerably when one gets up and about and that's the thing to do – rise, leave the cares between the sheets, make a cup of tea, still better, take an early-morning walk or, best of all, listen to or sing the odd chant!

'O Lux Beata Trinitas' is one chant which we can pin down firmly in terms of authorship – it was apparently written by one man – a saint – St Ambrose. At this point I'm pondering: so what is a saint anyway? I've just looked it up in the dictionary and there are three definitions:

1. a person who after death is formally recognised by a Christian Church as having attained a specially exalted place in heaven entitling him to veneration
2. a person of exceptional holiness
3. the collective body of those who are righteous in God's sight.

Now we can presume that the first description applies to all those standard saints with a capital S. But the last two could, with a push, include you too I'm sure!

I love the uncomplicated explanation of editor Donald Attwater in his

Introduction to the invaluable *Penguin Dictionary of Saints*:

> Sainthood – or any other degree of truly Chris-
> tian life – is not achieved by anyone's unaided
> efforts. It may be consciously taken as an ideal
> to be aimed at; it cannot be adopted and pur-
> sued as a 'career'. Men and women become
> saints by living 'in Christ', in whatever state of
> life to which they are called. They are enabled
> to do this by grace, the divine help – as Chris-
> tians believe – which Christ freely offers to every
> man according to the circumstances, capacities,
> and needs of each one. The saints are those who
> accept and cooperate with grace more whole-
> heartedly and more selflessly than do others, to
> a superlative degree: they become Christ-like
> through the help Christ gives them.

Where would we be without saints! Here's my personal Litany of the Saints!

St Jude, the patron of hopeless cases. *Pray for us!*
St Anne, to pray nine 'Hail Marys' to on Tuesday before twelve midday
for a surprise! *Pray for us!*
St Blaise, whose feastday it is on 3 February, patron saint of the throat;
and of wild animals too! *Pray for us!*
St Brighid, matron of healing, poetry and smithscraft. *Guí orainn!*
St Cecilia, matron of musicians, whom I had worn out every year during
my teens when I was doing music examinations! *Ora pro nobis!*

St Christopher guided us on our way when travelling, but St Colmcille
would definitely speed our journey on any Thursday. *Orate pro nobis!*

And do you remember the little cant we had to St Anthony when things
went missing?

St Anthony, St Anthony, please look around.
My .... is lost and it cannot be found!

And we promised him money too!

But it is St Mary of Magdala who has inspired many, many poets down through the ages. Two of them – Pádraic Pearse and Christina Rossetti – wrote Magdalen poems which tend to run in to each other in my mind. Both chose to structure their thoughts in five four-line stanzas, but I imagine that apart from sharing praises for Mary M. here, they might not have had that much to say to each other! I'm carefully balancing gender representation here for you also in the spirit that pervades this chant collection – the union of opposites!

Christina Rossetti (1830-1894) was almost a recluse, a minor Emily Dickinson-type figure in English poetry.

> She came in deep repentance,
> And knelt down at His feet
> Who can change the sorrow into joy,
> The bitter into sweet.
>
> She had cast away her jewels
> And her rich attire,
> And her breast was filled with a holy shame,
> And her heart with a holy fire.
>
> Her tears were more precious
> Than her precious pearls –
> Her tears that fell upon His feet
> As she wiped them with her curls.
>
> Her youth and her beauty
> Were budding to their prime;
> But she wept for the great transgression,
> The sin of other time.
>
> Trembling betwixt hope and fear,
> She sought the King of Heaven,
> Forsook the evil of her ways,
> Loved much, and was forgiven.

Pádraic Pearse (1879-1916) picks up gracefully on the relationship between Christ and Magdalen in a poem which is to be spoken out more than read. So off you go!

> O woman of the gleaming hair,
> (Wild hair that won men's gaze to thee)
> Weary thou turnest from the common stare,

For the shuiler Christ is calling thee.

O woman of the snowy side,
Many a lover hath lain with thee,
Yet left thee sad at the morning tide,
But thy lover Christ shall comfort thee.

O woman with the wild thing's heart,
Old sin hath set a snare for thee:
In the forest ways forspent thou art
But the hunter Christ shall pity thee.

O woman spendthrift of thyself,
Spendthrift of all the love in thee,
Sold unto sin for little pelf,
The captain Christ shall ransom thee.

O woman that no lover's kiss
(Tho' many a kiss was given thee)
Could slake thy love, is it not for this
The hero Christ shall die for thee?

Ave Verum

A ~ ve ve-rum Corpus na-tum de Ma-rí-a Vír-gi-ne:

Ve ~ re pas-sum immo-lá-tum in cru-ce pro hó-mi-ne.

Cu ~ jus la-tus per-fo-rá ~ tum

flu-xit a-qua et sán-gui-ne:

Es-to no ~ bis præ-gus-tá ~ tum

mor-tis in ex ~ á ~ mi-ne.

O Je ~ su dul-cis! O Je-su pi ~ e!

O Je ~ su Fi-li Ma-rí ~ æ!

AVE VERUM

On the seventh day God completed the work he had
been doing. He rested on the seventh day. God
blessed the seventh day and made it holy.

Genesis 2:2-3

Ave Verum Corpus
natum de María
Vírgine:
Vere passum, immolátum in
cruce pro hómine.
Cujus latus perforátum fluxit
aqua et sánguine:
Esto nobis praegustátum
mortis in exámine.
O Jesu dulcis!
O Jesu pie!
O Jesu Fíli Maríae.

Hail true body, born of
the Virgin Mary.
You truly suffered and were
sacrificed on the cross for
man. From your pierced side
flowed water and blood.
May you be our sustenance
before the ordeal of our death.
O sweet Jesus! O merciful
Jesus! O Jesus son of Mary!

MEDITATION

Seven times daily I praise you
for your righteous rulings.

Psalm 119:164

Seven musically simple outcries from the heart create this little chant.

Whether it be from the tradition here of Gregorian Chant, from my own Irish tradition of religious song, or indeed many other traditions, I feel there is a strong and ancient bond with the number seven. Numerical carols such as 'Seacht nDólás na Maighdine Muire' (The Seven Sorrows of Mary) and 'Seacht Suáilcí na Maighdine Muire' (The Seven Rejoices of Mary), collected from singers all over Ireland, are the oldest songs from the Irish tradition and come from the same soul-source and inspiration as Gregorian Chant.

Consider that number seven for a moment. How many important elements are defined in terms of groupings of seven? Here are some off the top of the head, as we say, and I'm sure you'll think of more yourself:
- seven days of the week
- seven deadly sins
- seven books of Wisdom
- seven seas
- seven continents.

From the biblical tradition of my favourite Gospel, John's:
- seven signs or miracles of Christ
- seven 'I am' sayings

From the Eastern tradition:
- seven chakras
- seven-year life cycles.

The Sufi poet Attar, in his mystical poem, 'The Colloquy of the Birds', describes the spiritual pilgrimage as the journey through the 'Seven Valleys'.

Last but not least, in music there are the seven notes in the Western musical scale – the seven notes of the river of Gregorian Chant through which we gloriously flow in song and praise!

Incidentally, it is interesting to go back over your own life to consider yourself at seven, fourteen, twenty-one, twenty-eight, thirty-five and so on. For me, certainly, the most dramatic points of my life fall easily into this pattern: at seven, I started singing lessons which were to shape my whole vocal journey; at twenty-one, I became engaged, to marry a year later; at twenty-eight, I started to carry my first child, recorded for the first time, and finished an MA programme on religious song, the genesis of what you read now!

As a singer and lover of all traditions of spiritual song, it can sometimes be uncanny when these traditions become interchangeable and merge into a feeling beyond spirituality, beyond music, and even as I try to explain it now, beyond words.

Just looking at the musical shape of this inspired little chant, 'Ave Verum', will illustrate what I'm trying to paint verbally. Musically, this is a real gem. If you look at the visual icon here of the music, you'll see that five of the seven phrases end with the same two long notes – ray and doh. A phrase, incidentally, is like a breath, a sentence, defined by a thread above the stave, almost like a daisy-chain where the daisies, the notes, are delicately bonded together in a never-ending circle, and each phrase or daisy-chain stands firmly and cheekily on its own in history.

If I were describing such musical architecture to you without you hearing it, you could not be blamed for imagining it to be dull and tedious. But nothing could be further from the truth and I pray that our singing of it here, although far from cold, calculating musical perfection, will, in some way, be different for every one of you, reflecting the seventh heaven of above and below!

This anonymous fourteenth-century hymn is traditionally sung at the Eucharist, a word which comes from Latin and Greek sources meaning the 'giving of thanks' – the act of thanksgiving. Within the Roman Catholic liturgy, the Eucharist forms the final moments where people share the eucharistic bread – *panis angelorum*, 'bread of angels' – and at the same time give thanks. So all are gathered together at that moment and, united spiritually in gratitude, become 'companions'.

Incidentally, the word 'friend' comes from the Germanic word *frijaz* which has two meanings. Wait for it! One is 'beloved', and the other is 'free', not in bondage! If only we could line up and balance these two concepts of love and freedom, if only we could generously offer this double-sided coin of companionship, it doesn't require too much vision to see that there would be far fewer acrimonious relationships on this planet.

As a final celebration of hymns of praise to Christ – a celebration of thanksgiving, of companionship — we turn to a prayer-poem written by English poet George Herbert, who died in 1633. He said that his time spent in prayer and in listening to cathedral music elevated his soul and was his Heaven upon Earth.

> Love bade me welcome; yet my soul drew back,
> Guilty of dust and sin.
> But quick-eyed Love, observing me grow slack
> From my first entrance in,
> Drew nearer to me, sweetly questioning
> If I lack'd anything.
> 'A guest,' I answer'd, 'worthy to be here:'
> Love said, 'You shall be he.'
> 'I, the unkind, ungrateful? Ah, my dear,
> I cannot look on Thee.'
> Love took my hand and smiling did reply,
> 'Who made the eyes but I?
> 'Truth, Lord, but I have marr'd them: let my shame
> Go where it doth deserve.'
> 'And know you not,' says Love, 'Who bore the blame?'
> 'My dear, then I will serve.'
> 'You must sit down,' says Love, 'and taste my meat.'
> So I did sit and eat.
>
> George Herbert

THE
GREATEST
ORNAMENT

LITURGY

The Church knew what the Psalmist knew:
Music praises God. Music is well or better able to
praise Him than the building of the church and all
its decoration; it is the Church's greatest ornament.

Igor Stravinsky, *Conversations with Stravinsky*

The word 'liturgy', the dictionary tells us, comes from the Greek
leitourgia, which means both 'a public service' and 'worship of the
gods'. Singing has come and gone in this liturgy story over the
centuries, sometimes enhancing, sometimes doing just the opposite!
I, like many others, feel deep down in my bones that Gregorian Chant
can restore what has become dull and lifeless, not just to its former
self but way, way beyond. It can also anchor worship in real dignity,
where true respect for spiritual values and for the 'otherness' of each
other is possible. These following liturgical chants sing of those
moments of recognition and integration. Heartwork, first and
foremost, governed my initial choice of fifty or so chants from the
vast sea of Mass chant. Headwork then whittled this body down again
by carefully choosing a popular, readily accessible decade of
music-prayers, which I present to you now.

Kyrie Eleison XVI

Kýrie, e-léison. Kýrie, e-léison.

Christe, e-léison. Christe, e-léison.

Kýrie, e-léison. Kýrie, e-léison.

Kyrie eléison,
Christe eléison,
Kyrie eléison.

Lord have mercy, Christ have mercy, Lord have mercy.

Kyrie Eleison
Missa pro Defunctis

Kýrie, e léison. *thrice*

Christe, e léison *thrice*

Kýrie, e léison. *twice*

Kýrie, e léison.

Have mercy on me, O God, in your goodness

Psalm 51:3

MEDITATION

Kyrie is the Greek trisyllabic cornerstone of Christian worship. This exclamatory cry for mercy has appeared in all Easter liturgies from the fourth century up to this day. It was spread by a Spanish pilgrim nun called Egeria, who visited Jerusalem about the year AD 380. She enthused about it in a letter to her sisters. It was introduced into the Roman liturgy by Pope Gelasius at the end of the fifth century.

It is surely this element of re-visitation of the past which is at the kernel of the healing grace of music. Music generally has such a power – the power of restoring memory and experience, the power of a recall of feeling totally beyond our control. In fact, recent research indicates that music elicits a greater response in Alzheimer's patients than does speech.

My first liturgical chant choice – the 'Kyrie' from Mass XVI – I love for its final phrase which takes you totally by surprise with the advent of a brand new note, an unexpected flattened note so novel and enchanting when all the other phrases end on the same note. Magic!

Incidentally, the traditional manner of performing any 'Kyrie' was to sing each Kyrie and each Christe *three* times, then sing the Kyrie three times again, with the final repeat usually altered as in the second 'Kyrie' here, from the Missa de Profunctis(Mass XVIII). We follow this plan as we sing this poignant plea for help. Despite its seeming simplicity, there is an ingenious programme in this piece, where the first three Kyries, the three Christes and the next two of the final set of Kyries all share the same step-wise, five-note phrase. But suddenly, the flower blossoms and the very final calling on the Lord to have mercy startlingly begins on the highest note yet in the chant! Then a leap of five notes down, five notes up again and then a higher note still! And to add to the work of art, the final *eleison* appears as before, bringing the ecstasy to an hypnotic close. Inspired!

As we recorded this particular 'Kyrie', we experimented. With just one microphone open beside the altar in the chapel, we gathered in a circle around the ambo at the other end. Paul intones the first Kyrie; I couldn't help joining in for the second, and the third Kyrie is a 'free for all'! And so on, through the triple Christe and the final Kyrie. So turn up the level controls, oil up your Greek, and give it your almighty best with us the third time round!

When I teach this chant in workshops, I love to get people to draw the outlines on paper, making the sound pattern visual as well as aural. You could try this by following the up-and-down movement of the music with your hand in the air, and you'll find that it gives a whole new three-dimensional feel to this age-old chant. It could become a dance-song meditation! Why not?

Qui tol- lis pec-cá - ta mun-di sús-ci - pe
de-pre -ca- ti - ó -nem no — strum.
Qui se-des ad déx-te-ram Patris, mi-se-ré-re no-bis.
Quó-ni-am tu so-lus sanctus. Tu so-lus Do-mi- nus.
Tu so-lus Al-tis-si -mus, Je - su Chri-ste
Cum Sanc-to Spí ~ ri-tu, in gló-ri -a De ~ i
Pa ~ tris. A — men.

And suddenly with the angel there was
a great throng of the heavenly host,
praising God and singing:
'Glory to God in the highest heaven,
and peace to men on whom his favour rests'.

Luke 2:13-14

GLORIA

Glória in excélsis Deo. Et in terra pax homínibus bonae voluntátis.

Laudámus te.

Benedícimus te.

Adorámus te.

Glorificámus te.

Grátias ágimus tibi propter magnam glóriam tuam.

Dómine Deus Rex caeléstis, Deus Pater omnípotens.

Dómine Fili unigénite Jesu Christe.

Dómine Deus, Agnus Dei, Fílius Patris.

Qui tollis peccáta mundi, miserere nobis.

Qui tollis peccáta mundi, súscipe deprecatiónem nostram.

Qui sedes ad dexteram Patris, miserére nobis.

Quóniam tu solus sanctus.

Tu solus Dóminus.

Tu solus Altíssimus Jesu Christe.

Cum Sancto Spíritu, in glória Dei Patris. Amen.

Glory to God in the highest. And peace to his people on earth. We praise you. We bless you. We adore you. We glorify you. We give you thanks for your great glory. Lord God, Heavenly King, Almighty God and Father. Lord Jesus Christ, only Son of the Father, Lord God, Lamb of God. You take away the sins of the world, have mercy on us. You take away the sins of the world, hear our prayer. You are seated at the right hand of the Father, have mercy on us. For you alone are the Holy One. You alone are the Lord. You alone are the Most High, Jesus Christ. With the Holy Spirit, in the glory of God the Father. Amen.

Gloria
Ambrosian

Gló-ri-a in ex-cél-sis De-o.

Et in ter-ra pax ho-mí-ni-bus bo-næ vo-lun-tá-tis.

Lau-dá-mus te. Be-ne-dí-cimus te. A-do-rá-mus te.

Glo-ri-fi-cá-mus te. Grá-ti-as á-gi-mus ti-bi

prop-ter mag-nam gló-ri-am tu-am. Dó-mi-ne

De-us Rex cæ-lés-tis, De-us Pa-ter om-ní-po-tens.

Dó-mi-ne Fi-li uni-gé-ni-te, Je-su Chris-te

Dó-mi-ne De-us, Ag-nus De-i, Fí-li-us Pa-tris. Qui tol-lis

pec-cá-ta mun-di,   mi-se-ré-re no-bis.

Qui tol-lis pec-cá-ta mundi,   sús-ci-pe

de-pre-ca-ti-ó-nem nos-tram. Qui se-des ad dex-te-ram
Pa-tris, mi-se-ré-re no-bis. Quó-ni-am tu so-lus sanc-tus.
Tu so-lus Dó-mi-nus. Tu so-lus Al-tís-simus Je-su
Chris-te. Cum Sancto Spí-ri-tu, in
gló-ri-a De-i Pa-tris. A-men.

MEDITATION

'The Gloria is part of a short series of very ancient hymns which can be traced back to the primitive Church, modelled on the psalms and a continuation of the tradition of the hymns of the New Testament.' So writes A.G. Martimor in a captivating account of the Eucharist, called *The Church at Prayer – The Eucharist.* (This book is all the more important and relevant to me because it was translated by two people not unconnected with this very book: Rev. Austin Flannery OP, who writes the Foreword here, and Fr Vincent Ryan OSB, former librarian in Glenstal Abbey, who generously and gently welcomed me many, many times to that library.) From this same source I learn that the oldest Latin text is found in a precious Irish manuscript from the seventh century called Antiphonarium Benchorensis, The Bangor Antiphonary.

Here we sing two of the many settings of the 'Gloria in Excelsis Deo'. The Ambrosian one (the second) is my favourite, but, probably for nostalgic as well as for musical reasons, I felt compelled to include also the Gloria from what's called the Missa de Angelis, 'The Mass of the Angels'. This Mass, Number VIII, was extremely popular in the past, and I'm sure it will jog the chant memory for any of you out there in your forties, fifties, and over.

As you can see from the scriptural reference above, it was the angels who first sang this song of praise!

> Music is well said to be the speech of angels.
>
> Thomas Carlyle

We are living in the angel era! There are representations of angels on everything – books, postcards, young girls' hairbands, garden furniture! Angels are in! And a friend of mine informed me recently that he could sense no less that seven (and you know my seven fixation) angels in my aura!

Well, let me tell you they weren't doing much yesterday, or else there's one terribly mischievous one among them who, as we say, had a field day! Last evening, after I had spent at least eight hours before this computer, gathering my scattered thoughts together, a friend of mine dropped by. In the enthusiasm of companionship, I forgot to save my day's endeavour! Ten minutes later we had a power failure! All the day's hard-earned thoughts *gone*! So it was back to the drawing-board last night and up at cock-crow – and I know well when that is because I have three of them running around crowing outside! Still not having learned my saving lesson, on the computer I mean, at around 2pm just as I started to muse on angels again, the incredible happened. Another flash power failure *just* at the same point! Honestly, there isn't a hint of exaggeration here! Perhaps God called back his angels just at that moment – as happened to Emily Dickinson one fantastic evening in her poetic memory:

> God permits industrious Angels –
> Afternoon – to play –
> I met one – forgot my Schoolmates –
> All – for this – straightway –
>
> God calls home – the Angels – promptly
> At the Setting Sun–
> I missed mine – how *dreary*– Marbles –
> After playing *Crown*!
>
> Emily Dickinson

I recall, through a rather troubled, lonely childhood, having a special relationship with my guardian angel. Many of you will remember the morning and night prayer which I certainly never forgot to say then:

> O angel of God, my guardian dear,
> To whom God's love commits me here;
> Ever this day/night be at my side,
> To light and guard, to rule and guide. Amen.

My guardian angel was a 'him', I think! My mother used to tell us, playfully of course, that there were two reasons or signs why God, heaven, the angels and all of that were male: one reason is because a holy song is called a 'hymn', and secondly all these hymns end with A-men!

While you listen here to this longer-than-usual chant, Gloria VIII, let me tell you more of the moods and auras that crossed my mind as I sang it. I can never think on this chant without remembering a dear friend who was parish priest of Adare, County Limerick for many years. Our friendship began when we met on an international Gregorian Chant programme in France, led by chant scholar Mary Berry, twenty-two years ago. Over the two weeks, we lived Gregorian Chant, sharing and learning chants from one another, visiting Solesmes, the Benedictine monastery renowned for its chant books, and for its interpretation of neumes and notes.

Father John, Father Des, my husband Mick and I became the unofficial Irish entertainers of the group! Incidentally, Mick and I were on our honeymoon, and from this school we went on to partake in the disciplined prayer routine of the ecumenical community in Taizé. Then, shattering all our sombre spirits, we ended our *mí na meala*, 'honey-month' as it is called in Irish, at a crazy, uproarious folk music festival in Brittany! A catholic (with a small c) all-inclusive honeymoon!

Fr John would ring regularly over the next seven years wondering 'if there was any news'! 'Well, you know, Fr John is always praying for you and sure, it won't be long now,' became the familiar message. So when I did begin to carry Eoin, no doubt was allowed in any mind but that it was Fr John's storming heaven and the Holy Spirit that Eoin had not lost his way! I'm sure this story will ring bells for some readers! Eoin was baptised in Adare in May 1980.

Father John asked Mick and myself over to hear his church choir one evening, soon after the French connection. They were all gathered together in the choir loft of that most extraordinarily atmospheric cathedral there.

This Gloria VIII was one of the pieces he wanted us to hear. And, having established a level of concentration and attention from the choir – a level which was palpable – he shouted at them, 'After four!' Then raising his hands to conduct this Gloria, he shouted again, this time just 'Four!' After a further interval which bore absolutely no relationship to the count-in, the choir began what was a very moving, competent rendering of Gloria VIII! Another absurd example of the timelessness of Gregorian Chant!

My earliest memories of singing this sixteenth-century Gloria go back to primary school days when, note-for-note, this beautiful chant was imprinted indelibly on my memory. Mind you, we rarely or never hit on the high prayer points which lie deep in these songs, but God bless all those teachers who meticulously preserved these chants anyhow!

In musical theory, we call this type of chant 'through-composed', which means that all the phrases differ and each lofty concept of worship sings with its own voice and notes. From among the many musical gems of this piece, my favourite is the final Amen which has no less than *seven* notes as a final outcry of praise! What a wonderful sweep to the music; the angels sing their hearts out here.

The Ambrosian Gloria has been dated to the twelfth century, eight centuries later than the fourth century St Ambrose. The very simple declamatory style of music is broken gloriously five times with a flourish of notes at the end of a phrase which seems to go on forever.

But there's a whole richness of musical architecture within these fanfares: there's a basic plan of a dozen notes held together but on the two phrases praising Jesus Christ, one note extra is woven, unnoticed at the beginning, the baker's dozen, or is it Ambrose's dozen? The entire chant dances around five notes, from soh to high re, but the dance culminates in an Amen, as in Gloria VIII. This is spell-binding because it now dances around a new pattern of five notes ending on the lowest note – nothing more needs to be said!

Alleluia!
Praise God in his Temple on earth.

Psalm 150, final chorus of praise

As these exclamations ring through my being just now, I'm back in San Francisco four years ago. One sunny evening (though nobody comments on the endless sun-filled days there and indeed, after a while, the predictability of the weather becomes boring, particularly to us Irish where the four seasons could conceivably appear over two hours of any day!), I was singing at a seventieth birthday celebration of an amazing mystic, potter, writer, poet and friend, M. C. Richards. Taking part in that occasion was the world-acclaimed, contemporary classical composer, John Cage. On hearing that I was Irish he asked me if I had known Joe Heaney (Seosamh Ó hÉanaí), the legendary *sean-nós* singer from Connemara, and I immediately struck up: *Agus aililiú lá, 'gus aililiú ló, aililiú ló 'gus ó* because I had learned this song from the singing of Joe. Before I had finished the chorus, John was weeping. He had been very close to Joe when he was alive and had written him into his composition *Roaratorio*. When I got back home to Murroe where I then lived, the phone rang one evening. 'This is John Cage. Do you remember me?' Did I what! He had been a text-book figure and a god to me ever since student days in University College Cork. He invited me to be the singer in *Roaratorio* the following month, and that experience plus singing at a memorial ritual in New York to mark his own passing away a short time later, are two memories that I will always cherish. To the memory of John and Joe, I dedicate these little chants. *Go ndéana Dia trócaire orthu, beirt!* (May the Lord have mercy on them both.)

The word 'Alleluia', an expression of sheer joy, we've come to take so much for granted. It derives from two Hebrew words *halelú jáh* which mean 'praise ye God'. *Halelú* comes from *hala* which means 'to shine'! *Jáh* is God, slightly reminiscent of our own Irish word for God, *Dia*. Through Greek and Latin versions of this word, it comes to us now as Alleluia.

It's a heavenly word to sing on, probably because of all the vowel sounds within it broken up only by the most magical of all the consonants, 'L'. It flows out unbroken, a prayerful out-pouring.

I have chosen three Alleluias here which traditionally would have been sung before the Gospel reading as a welcoming light to shine through the reader onto the sacred page and into the hearts of the listener. A three-fold process which demands by its very nature the utmost dedication and detachment, all at the one time. By singing these Alleluias – particularly the first, the easiest and most accessible – we take our part in the drama of the Word. In that drama, balance is of the essence, and that balance creates an internal dialogue between the two primary key systems of our classical music heritage. Alleluias one and three are in a major key while Alleluia two is neatly placed between them. An Alleluia sandwich!

What pure music flows out of these Alleluias – a whole aural symphony in just thirteen seconds as I sing through one of them now! Thirteen seconds of pure light!

Credo III

Cre-do in u-num De- um.

Pa-trem om-ni-po-tén-tem, fac-tó-rem cœ-li et ter-ræ,

vi-si-bí-li- um óm-ni-um, et in-vi-si-bí- li-um,

Et in u-num Dó-mi-num Je-sum Chris-tum Fi-li-

um De-i u-ni-gé-ni-tum. Et ex Pa-tre na-tum

an-te óm-ni-a sæ-cu-la. De-um de De-o,

lumen de lu-mi-ne, De-um ve-rum de De-o ve-ro.

Gé-ni-tum, non fac-tum, con-sub-stan-ti-á-lem Pa-tri

per quem óm-ni-a fac-ta sunt. Qui prop-ter nos

hó-mi-nes, et prop-ter nostram salú-tem des-cén-dit

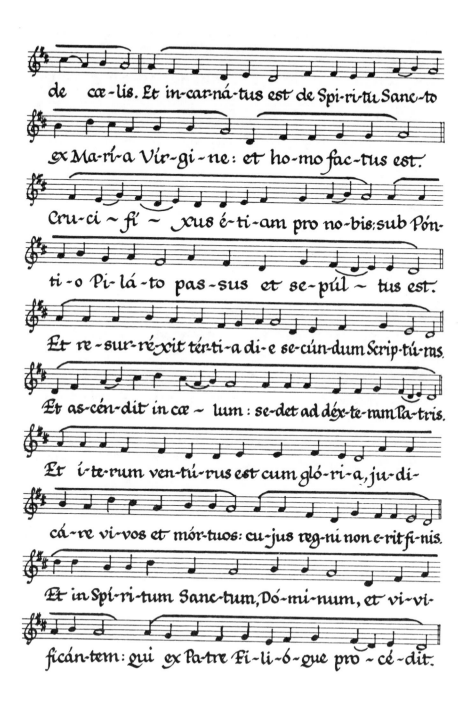

de cœ-lis. Et in-car-ná-tus est de Spi-ri-tu Sanc-to

ex Ma-rí-a Vír-gi-ne: et ho-mo fac-tus est.

Cru-ci ~ fí ~ xus é-ti-am pro no-bis; sub Pón-

ti-o Pi-lá-to pas-sus et se-púl ~ tus est.

Et re-sur-ré-xit tér-ti-a di-e se-cún-dum Scrip-tú-ras.

Et as-cén-dit in cœ ~ lum: se-det ad déx-te-ram Pa-tris.

Et í-te-rum ven-tú-rus est cum gló-ri-a, ju-di-

cá-re vi-vos et mór-tuos: cu-jus reg-ni non e-rit fi-nis.

Et in Spí-ri-tum Sanc-tum, Dó-mi-num, et vi-vi-

fi-cán-tem: qui ex Pa-tre Fi-li-ó-que pro ~ cé-dit.

Qui cum Patre et Fi-li-o si-mul ado-rá-tur et con-glo-ri-fi-cá-tur: qui lo-cú-tus est per pro-phé-tas. Et u-nam sanc-tam ca-thó-li-cam et a-pos-tó-li-cam Ec-clé-si-am. Con-fí-te-or u-num bap-tís-ma in re-mis-si-ó-nem pec-ca-tó-rum. Et ex-spec-to re-sur-rec-ti-ó-nem mor-tu-ó-rum. Et vi-tam ven-tú-ri sǽ-cu-li. A men.

Credo ut intelligam –
I do not seek to understand so that I can believe,
but I believe so that I may understand;
and what is more,
I believe that unless I do believe,
I shall not understand.

St Anselm (1033-1109)

CREDO III

Credo in unum Deum,
Patrem omnipoténtem,
factórem caeli et terrae,
visibílium ómnium, et
invisíbilium.
Et in unum Dóminum Jesum
Christum Filium Dei
unigénitum.
Et ex Patre natum ante ómnia
saecula.
Deum de Deo, lumen de
lumine, Deum verum de
Deo vero.
Génitum, non factum,
consubstantiálem Patri
per quem ómnia facta sunt.
Qui propter nos hómines, et
propter nostram salútem
descéndit de caelis.
Et incarnátus est de Spiritu
Sancto ex María Vírgine:
et homo factus est.
Crucifíxus étiam pro nobis:
sub Póntio Piláto passus et
sepúltus est.
Et ressuréxit tértia die,
secúndum Scriptúras.
Et ascéndit in caelum:
sedet ad déxteram Patris.
Et íterum ventúrus est cum
glória, iudicáre vivos et
mórtuos:
cujus regni non erit finis.
Et in Spíritum Sanctum,
Dóminum, et vivificántem:

I believe in one God,
Father Almighty, maker of
heaven and earth, of all that
is seen and unseen. And in
one Lord, Jesus Christ, the
only Son of God eternally
begotten of the Father. God
from God, Light from Light,
true God from true God.
Begotten, not made, of one
Being with the Father:
through Him all things were
made. For us men and for our
salvation he came down from
Heaven. And by the power
of the Holy Spirit, he became
incarnate from the Virgin
Mary: And was made man.
For our sake he was crucified:
under Pontius Pilate he
suffered and died. And on the
third day, he rose again in
accordance with the
Scriptures. And ascended into
heaven: seated at the right
hand of the Father. And he
will come again in glory to
judge the living and the dead:
and his kingdom will have no
end. And in the Holy Spirit,
the Lord, the giver of life:
who proceeds from the Father

qui ex Patre Filióque procédit.
Qui cum Patre et Fílio simul
adorátur et conglorificátur:
qui locútus est per prophétas.
Et unam sanctam cathólicam
et apostólicam Ecclésiam.
Confíteor unum baptísma in
remissiónem peccatórum.
Et exspecto resurrectiónem
mortuórum.
Et vitam ventúri saéculi.
Amen.

worshipped and glorified:
who has spoken through the
Prophets. And in one holy
catholic and apostolic Church.
I believe in one baptism for
the forgiveness of sins. And I
look for the resurrection of the
world to come. Amen.

MEDITATION

A chant of belief. To believe in someone, something, God, ourselves, what does it actually mean? Is my belief any different to yours? Can a belief be a half-truth? And could that half-truth be the wrong half, if you know what I mean?

The word stems from late Old English words meaning to 'hold dear' or 'to trust in'. So to believe means to love, really, and a belief is inspired by someone or something. A belief is a poem, a song and right now, I want to share one of my 'beliefs' with you.

Some months ago, Mick and I stole away for one of those occasional moments of being together and apart from the world! We headed for East Cork for that one precious, disengaged, free night. An overtreasured time, though so much so that in the frenzy of savouring the space, I was wide-eyed at five in the morning!

So I slipped out from under the bedclothes as quietly as I could and headed for the nearby strand of Ballycotton. There the belief – the memory I will forever hold dear and trust in, began. Belief in the interconnectedness of everything – of God, nature, beauty, life itself – all these took the form of a poem. Now like many of you readers, I *never* in my life before wrote a poem. Poetry, the song of the poet, and the poet-person had always occupied a privileged, untouchable room in my heart, and always will, I pray. But this was different. This was a poem for myself, about myself and it *had* to be written down. I will never forget the appeasement that followed, a calm and total trust in beholding God's finger on the rising sun that early morning. I'm sharing it now not out of any belief in its poetic merit only to urge you to 'grasp the nettle' yourself. Go on – write your first poem now! If I can do it, you can!

ONE FOR SORROW

Eyes to see – hearts to feel
Far-out sun yawning before the rock face.
Credo in Unum Deum
Now a burning ball admiring your own
face in the watery mirror
Lead, kindly light.
Mr and Mrs Magpie fly before your
Face –
One for Sorrow –
Two for Joy.
Who would fall for
my witness of your
Rise!
Seeing is believing – believing is singing.
Will you sing for me – Mrs Magpie?
Chatter out into the ocean
A different rhythm to my chattering
teeth of fear
of
One for Sorrow –

Ballycotton Beach, 5 May 1996, 5.50am

A stone's throw from Ballycotton strand is the picturesque village of Baile Mhac Oda in the undulating, luscious land of county Cork. Years ago, I was a disciple of a traditional singer from there called Seosamh Mac Shamhráin. His stocky build, his heavy-featured face, seemed to me then to be part and parcel of the mounds of earth and stones around him. From him I imbibed a traditional, *sean-nós* Credo in Irish which I'm sure was around among those same stones long before the seventeenth-century version which I sing for you here! This Gregorian Credo is one of the finest settings from the plain-chant wellsprings. Just look at the Amen; there are sixteen notes on the first 'A'.

Like the Gregorian Gloria VIII of the century before, this Credo plays around the third note – mi. All of the nineteen beautiful through-composed phrases in this piece, including the Amen, begin on either soh, mi or doh – eleven on soh, four on mi, four on doh. Singing with an open fifth drone, I love interacting with that triad.

Look at the phrase 'and He ascended into heaven'. The music mirrors the action – word-painting or 'programme music' we call it. Here it starts on the lowest note of the piece, then sweeps up the octave to a little triple note, like an ornament, on *caelo*. Look also at the Amen – the full range, a difficult one to sing. As in the Gloria Amen, it must spring from you like a beautiful flower!

Sanctus XVIII

Sanc-tus, Sanc-tus, Sanc-tus Dómi-nus De-us Sá-ba-oth.

Ple-ni sunt cœ-li et ter-ra gló-ri-a tu-a. Ho-sán-na in excélsis.

Be - ne-díc-tus qui ve - nit in nó-mi-ne Dó-mi-ni.

Ho-sán- na in ex-cél- sis.

See now, your king comes to you;
he is victorious, he is triumphant,
humble and riding on a donkey,
on a colt, the foal of a donkey.

Zechariah 9:9

Sanctus, Sanctus, Sanctus
Dóminus Deus Sábaoth.
Pleni sunt caeli et terra glória
tua.
Hosánna in excélsis.
Benedíctus qui venit in
nómine Dómini.
Hosánna in excélsis.

Holy, Holy, Holy
Lord, God of power
and might. Heaven and earth
are full of your glory.
Hosanna in the highest.
Blessed is He who comes in
the name of the Lord.
Hosanna in the highest.

MEDITATION

A colt, I always thought, was a male horse or pony, but all four gospels, including the Zechariah prophecy, above, very specifically mention a donkey.

Donkeys are sacred animals, still carrying and taking an equal share of that historic moment by the Mount of Olives when everybody burst into praise with these sanctified words. Let me tell you about my donkey! I had been travelling home last year on the thirteenth of March having sung at a really joyous and happy wedding in the historic, magical surroundings of Duiske Abbey in County Kilkenny. My mind was full of the 'chattering monkeys' again, and one stood out boldly and said: What about getting a donkey? A monkey wanting a donkey!!

Well, no sooner had the thought bubbled up than I looked to the right of me and there was a man by the side of the road tending to a donkey! So I stopped the car, turned back and said to him, 'Where will I get a donkey?' 'I'll get one for you, sure I know your face,' he said. 'You're the singer and I know where to get you a donkey!'

Three days later, on the nineteenth of March, the feast of St Joseph (who himself must have owned a donkey), Josie arrived. This day has always been special for me. It seems to restore normality after the St Patrick's holiday. It's a subdued, interior day always. So the latest arrival to our family *had* to be called Josie. Not just because I first laid eyes on her on the day that was in it but listen to this! Just as my donkey-finder was taking her out of the trailer, he said, 'Come on there, Josephine!' 'Why are you calling her that?' I asked. 'Ah! no reason at all,' he said. 'That name just came to me!'

Josie had been badly beaten so she had a chronic mistrust of people. However, I can report that after five months of nightly visits and chats, a dose of vitamins, healing cream for her sore eye, she zig-zags over to me the minute she hears the door opening!

G. K. Chesterton's poetry never moved me much. Possibly because I am a a singer, his description of the Irish people in 'The Ballad of the White Horse' makes me wince:

> For the great Gaels of Ireland
> Are the men that God made mad,
> For all their wars are merry,
> And all their songs are sad.

As Patrick Murray, editor of that invaluable treasury of Irish religious verse, *The Deer's Cry*, reacts: 'Wars are never merry – and Irish wars are no exception ... And not all the songs of the Gael are sad, though many of them are serious.'

Yet Chesterton's inspired homage to the donkey is with me every time I look into Josie's eyes, and every time I repeat it it helps me thank God for the beauty and presence of every single animal, bird and plant in this world of ours.

> When fishes flew and forests walked
> And figs grew upon thorn,
> Some moment when the moon was blood
> Then surely I was born;
>
> With monstrous head and sickening cry
> And ears like errant wings,
> The devil's walking parody
> On all four-footed things.
>
> The tattered outlaw of the earth,
> Of ancient crooked will;
> Starve, scourge, deride me: I am dumb,
> I keep my secret still.
>
> Fools! For I also had my hour;
> One far fierce hour and sweet:
> There was a shout about my ears,
> And palms before my feet.
>
> G.K. Chesterton

Pater Noster

PATER NOSTER

In your prayers do not babble ... your Father knows
what you need before you ask him. So you should
pray like this:

Matthew 6:7-9

Pater noster, qui es in
   caelis:
   sanctificétur nomen tuum;
advéniat regnum tuum;
fiat volúntas tua, sicut in caelo
   et in terra.
Panem nostrum cotidiánum
   da nobis hódie;
et dimítte nobis débita nostra
sicut et nos dimíttimus
   debitóribus nostris;
et ne nos indúcas in
   tentatiónem
sed líbera nos a malo.

Our Father, who art in
   heaven: hallowed be
thy name; Thy kingdom
come; Thy will be done on
earth as it is in heaven. Give
us this day our daily bread;
and forgive us our trespasses
as we forgive those who
trespass against us; and lead
us not into temptation, but
deliver us from evil.

MEDITATION

While the Sanctus and Agnus Dei throw up four-legged creature images, so
the 'Our Father', sandwiched in the middle of the two, has fowl connections
for me! When I was seven or eight, full of piety and precociousness, I felt
that my mother's hens should pray! So, unknowingly following the
instructions of the Lord on how to pray, I would go into my private room
(which was the henhouse) and when I had shut the door, I'd pray with the
hens! 'Our Father' was the prayer of the day!

   This became quite normal for them after a while and I think they even
began to look forward to Compline. The beady little eyes would flicker as

the crowing and the cackling of the daytime relaxed and wound down to a sympathetic hierarchy of hen-purring and me-babbling. Pater Noster! Had to be heard to be believed!

Well, as the years went on and my diligence wore off, the henfold, in my absence, forgot one evening to pray for their daily bread! My brother and I had been left minding and feeding the hens for a week. We forgot them and they all starved to death! A dark moment in my memory – and the dark moment of the 'Pater Noster' is mirrored in the music here where the lowest note sounds as a reminder to shun temptation and sin.

The next day, seeing Jesus coming towards him,
John said, 'Look, there is the lamb of God that takes
away the sin of the world.

John 1:29-30

AGNUS DEI XVIII

Agnus Dei, qui tollis peccáta mundi, miserére nobis.
Agnus Dei, qui tollis peccáta mundi, miserére nobis.
Agnus Dei, qui tollis peccáta mundi, dona nobis pacem.

Lamb of God, you take away the sins of the world, have mercy on us.
Lamb of God, you take away the sins of the world, have mercy on us.
Lamb of God, you take away the sins of the world, grant us peace.

MEDITATION

In this little piece we ask for mercy: 'Lord, be merciful to me, a sinner', which I sometimes render as 'Lord, be merciful to me a singer!' A very thin dividing line between sinning and singing! Just one letter! And we're all both sinners and singers!

But this little phrase is the well-known, often-quoted humble prayer from the parable of the tax collector in Luke's gospel. The moral tale ends with lines which always bring back the lofty concepts of the great Marian hymn, 'The Magnificat': 'For all who exalt themselves will be humbled, but those who humble themselves, will be exalted.'

And look at what this twelfth-century music is telling us here about sinning and singing! There are just four notes in play here. The lowest note is F, and this appears only on the word *peccata* – 'sins'. Like the 'Pater Noster' before, another musical example of sin dragging us down!

At Mass for the dead long ago, this little plea for mercy and peace for ourselves turned the prayer wheel around to pray intensely for the eternal peace of the dead one. I liked and miss this moment, and break the rules now and again myself when singing at the coffin of a friend or acquaintance!

'*Agnus Dei, qui tollis peccata mundi,*
dona eis requiem.'

'Lamb of God, you take away the sins of the world,
give her/him lasting rest and peace.'

A special moment in time, in life and in death, a tiny taste of the ultimate
peace that awaits us all.

St John the Baptist it was who, in the first chapter of his story, first labelled
Jesus the 'Lamb of God'. But Jesus sees himself as the Good Shepherd in that
superlative, moving, later Chapter Ten. I love this chapter for the stability, the
certainty of salvation it promises. At least five times, he assures us that he will
lay down his life for us his sheep. It's an awesome thought!

The sheep that belong to me listen to my voice.

John 10:27

This time last year, I had a sheep that belonged to me and listened to
my voice! Nonie, she was called. She had short legs because of some disease
which she'd had in her youth. But she was fine and sturdy, made all the more
so by my going out to feed her and Josie the donkey with the 'groodles' (what
we call the supper leftovers in our house!). Although I loved her dearly, I'm
afraid I wasn't the great shepherd, and so about eight months ago stray dogs
attacked her in the middle of the night and we found her dead the next day.
We buried our own little *agnus dei* that evening, with a chant or two in a
corner of the field behind us here!

SHEEP AND LAMBS

All in the April evening,
April airs were abroad;
The sheep with their little lambs
Passed me by on the road.

The sheep with their little lambs
Passed me by on the road;
All in the April evening
I thought on the Lamb of God.

Katharine Tynan

If you haven't already met her, I've been waiting to introduce you to
Katharine Tynan, author of this hymn of the fold. She draws together many
strands of common, shared thoughts for me in a way different yet similar to

Emily Dickinson – that old unity of opposites again!

Both women lived through twenty years of the nineteenth century together – between 1861 when Katharine was born to 1886 when Emily died – but on different sides of the Atlantic. Emily never completed her Mount Holyoke Seminary training and Katharine left school at fourteen; Katharine began her poetry-writing at seventeen; Emily too must have been building up her neatly-bound poetic bundle from this age; our Katharine married and had three children, Emily became a recluse; both women left behind most remarkable and important literature – letters, poems, novels, short stories.

It is now Katharine's turn to enfold us with her spirituality, with her meditations, when like Deutoronomy in the musical *Cats*, she points the finger of salvation to those who serve, deserve and listen. It's the month of April as I write. Ewes are mothering their sheep, protecting them above themselves. Katharine writes here as protector of her children, and, as any mother would, begs to be left with them until they're grown.

> I am the pillars of the house;
> The keystone of the arch am I,
> Take me away, and roof and wall
> Would fall to ruin utterly.
>
> I am the fire upon the hearth,
> I am the light of the good sun,
> I am the heat which warms the earth,
> Which else were colder than a stone.
>
> At me the children warm their hands;
> I am the light of love alive.
> Without me cold the hearthstone stands,
> Nor could the precious children thrive.
>
> I am the twist that holds together
> The children in its sacred ring,
> Their knot of love, from whose close tether
> No lost child goes a-wandering.
>
> I am their wall against all danger,
> Their door against the wind and snow,
> Thou Whom a woman laid in manger,
> Take me not till the children grow!
>
> Katharine Tynan

ITE MISSA EST

Jesus said to him, 'Go, and do the same yourself.'

Luke 10:37

Ite missa est.
Deo grátias.

Go, the Mass is ended.
Thanks be to God.

MEDITATION

An almost compulsive desire to attend Mass has been a constant memory etched in my being. Now, when I am at home, midday sees me motoring up the winding avenue of Glenstal Abbey, to be in chapel for community Mass there when time stands still and we wait for God, washed in the sound of Gregorian Chant. Wherever I am, I nearly always automatically, subconsciously become aware of the celebration of the Eucharist there at 12.10pm. God seems to stop me in my tracks to take that time out to be silent, to listen and to hear, to become like the traditional old owl of wisdom!

> A wise old owl sat in an oak
> The more he saw the less he spoke.
> The less he spoke the more he heard
> Why can't we all be like that bird?

I recall another silly old cant – but not totally irrelevant here as we sing these healing hymns – about three owls! Like the one above, it is written by the well known, nameless, ageless poet Anon!

This one is to be read aloud, deliberately, slowly and melodramatically!

> There were three little owls in a wood
> Who sang hymns whenever they could
> What the words were about
> You could never make out,
> But you felt it was doing them good!

The ideal task of any Mass is to let you arrive at the high doh of worship – double the sound-frequencies of low doh, and the nearest point to Heaven! And the whole Mass experience becomes intertwined with music, song and chant. But it's not always as simple or easy as this, coming out renewed at high doh, double the frequency at which we crawled in! A friend of mine who has no real interest in music says, 'Whether you reach or can sing high doh, the important thing is what you go out and *do*!' Of course, there's worship and there's worship, different kinds, different times, different souls. Let me bow out here, and leave you in the safe hands of Emily again – who never reached high doh in the sense of Mass attendance. Yet her Sabbath was a true Eucharist, an act of thanksgiving of a cosmic kind!

Some keep the Sabbath going to Church –
I keep it, staying at Home –
With a Bobolink for a Chorister –
And an Orchard, for a Dome –

Some keep the Sabbath in Surplice –
I just wear my Wings –
And instead of tolling the Bell, for Church,
Our little Sexton – sings.

God preaches, a noted Clergyman –
And the sermon is never long,
So instead of getting to Heaven, at last –
I'm going, all along.

Emily Dickinson

Three different settings, that musical sandwich again as in the Alleluias but this time the other way around, just to keep you on your toes! So here we have a major *Ite* (from the angelic 'Missa de Angelis', Missa VIII) sandwiched between two minors. All of them are major in the sense of being 'massive' prayers! I sang them 'by heart' the evening this recording was carried out. I hear now that as I closed my eyes and imagined the long grass swaying in the field which these chants paint for me, this beautiful final setting got the better of me – and what you see will not be exactly what you hear. So *ite* – go hastily on to chants of repose, and don't be too hard on me!

THE
FINAL JOURNEY

REQUIEM

Lux ætérna

Then the angel showed me the river of life,
rising from the throne of God and of the Lamb
and flowing crystal-clear down the middle of
the city street. On either side of the river were the
trees of life, which bear twelve crops of fruit in a year,
one in each month, and the leaves of which are
the cure for the heathens.

Revelation 22:1-2

ANTIPHON:

Lux aetérna lúceat eis,
Dómine,
cum sanctis tuis in aetérnum
quia pius es.
Réquiem aetérnam dona eis,
Dómine,
et lux perpétua lúceat eis.
cum sanctis tuis in aeternum
quia pius es.

May eternal light
shine upon
him/her, O Lord, with your
holy ones forever. Grant
him/her eternal rest, O Lord
and may perpetual light shine
upon him/her. With your
saints forever who are holy.

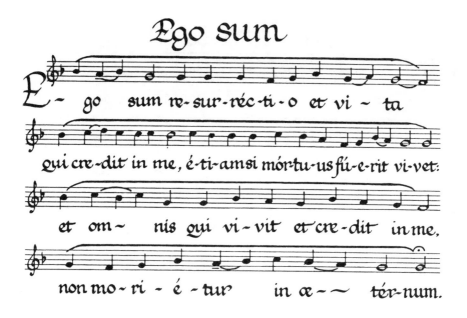

Ego sum

E - go sum re-sur-réc-ti-o et vi - ta
qui cre-dit in me, é-ti-am si mór-tu-us fú-e-rit vi-vet:
et om - nis qui vi - vit et cre-dit in me,
non mo - ri - é - tur in æ - ~ tér-num.

I am the Way, the Truth and the Life.

John 14:6

Ego sum resurréctio et vita
qui credit in me, étiam si
mórtuus fuérit vivet:
et omnis qui vivit et credit in
me, non moriétur in
aetérnum.

I am the resurrection and
the life: anyone who
believes in me lives: and all
who live and believe in me
will never die.

In Paradisum

In pa- ra- dí- sum de- dú- cant te án- ge- li:

in tu- o ad- vén- tu sus- cí- pi- ant te már- ty- res

et per- dú- cant te in ci- vi- tá- tem sanc- tam Je- rú- sa- lem.

Cho- rus an- ge- ló- rum te sus- cí- pi- at,

et cum Lá- za- ro quon- dam páu- pe- re

æ- tér- nam hábe- as ré- qui- em.

IN PARADISUM

And now I lift up my face
and to you I turn my eyes.
Let your word deliver me from earth.

Sarah's prayer for death, Tobit 3:12-14

In paradísum dedúcant te
ángeli:
in tuo advéntu suscípiant te
mártyres
et perdúcant te in civitátem
sanctam Jerúsalem.

Chorus angelórum te
suscípiat,
et cum Lázaro quondam
paupere aetérnam hábeas
réquiem.

May the angels lead
you into Paradise:
may the martyrs come to
welcome you and take you to
the holy city, the new
Jerusalem. May the chorus of
angels receive you and where
Lazarus is poor no longer,
may you find eternal rest.

MEDITATION

I felt a Funeral, in my Brain –
And mourners to and fro
Kept treading – treading – till it seemed
That Sense was breaking through –

And when they all were seated,
A service, like a Drum –
Kept beating – beating – till I thought
My mind was going numb –

And then I heard them lift a Box
And creak across my Soul
With those same Boots of Lead, again,
Then Space – began to toll,

As all the Heavens were a Bell,
And Being, but an Ear,
And I, and Silence, some strange Race
Wrecked, solitary, here –

And then a Plank in Reason, broke,
And I dropped down, and down –
And hit a World, at every plunge,
And Finished knowing – then –

Emily Dickinson

A strange and startling Dickinsonesque description of funerary obsequies. I'm sure you, like myself, are acutely aware of the coldness, the lack of reality, the almost inhuman way in which we cope nowadays with bereavement in our own lives and in the lives of others. The body (I always shudder when I say the word 'corpse') hastily carried away from the heart-home to the funeral home; family and friends shuffling past one another, shaking hands awkwardly and muttering, 'Sorry for your trouble.' I wonder who coined that silly word-quartet? How often do we sweep grief under the funeral-parlour carpet and leave the mourners to grieve alone?

How did we lose that wisdom of our elders to cry, to lament? To come out with the most basic of all human emotions – tears – the salt tears which flow from the heart up through the throat, cleansing us, healing us, irrigating the system, washing our grief right through us.

And indeed, as with singing, there are the two faces of tears: solitary tears which will flow spontaneously with a life of their own in the face of the deepest feelings of both joy and sorrow, and social tears which envelop and bathe those who are privileged to be around – and these can be the most therapeutic of all.

I will always remember a moment of being conscious and totally aware of these shared tears. My mother, in her eighties, fell and had to be hospitalised some four years ago. For me, believing that she would not recover, this was the time of letting go, of facing the ultimate loosening of the apron strings. So, one Saturday morning, I returned from the hospital, having forcefully camouflaged the sadness for three hours or more. Behind the closed home door I sobbed uncontrollably, not sensing that my eldest son, Eoin, who was twelve then, was there in the hallway with me. I will never forget the unfathomable look on his face when he came over and stood right beside me so that I could and could not feel him – with me and yet apart – with all his undefiled, unbridled child-wisdom. Again, that union of opposites – mother/son, youth/age, together/apart. I'm back there now, reaching for the nearby water font, dipping into it, blessing myself, blessing Eoin and the world on the other side of the front door through water, mingling human tears with tears of the spirit, bound together through the Sign of the Cross.

This flowing, manual gesture from the Christian tradition is much more than the symbolic ritual of making the cross-sign on oneself with water: it protects one's aura; it is a mingling of the senses and the four elements – earth, air, fire, and water – each element corresponding to the four body-points as the right hand traces the outline of the Celtic cross while we call on the name of the Father, co-ordinating word and gesture through the head, the intellect, the heavens. In the name of the Son – we point to the earth, the heart, the sensual. The name of the Holy Spirit incorporates east and west, the opposite poles. Amen – the final consent to the forces of light – culminates in a joining of hands, the ultimate sign of relief and release in God! This sign blesses my travels at home and abroad. At home for two reasons: firstly, I can *never* drive past a church without instinctively acknowledging a presence of the Other by blessing myself, a gesture which surprises many an unsuspecting passenger who has not been brought up with anything remotely like this habit! Secondly, and on a much more superstitious note, when a lone magpie happens to cross my path as I drive, to avoid the terrible fate of 'one for sorrow', I wish the magpie and its sorrowful baggage away by tracing the cross almost without thinking.

And as I travel abroad, I love to ferret out the airport chapel, making my entrance into this physical space for quiet and peace through forming the Sign of the Cross. It is such a sanctioned space – a space in which to observe other ways of worship, other people in worship, a privilege one rarely gets. Where else would you experience, as I have, an entire Jewish family – parents, grandparents and children – on a prayer mat sharing the Torah, the whole body of Jewish sacred writings; or a group of Africans, dressed in the brightest, most joyful colours in the world, praising God in dance, song, shouts and claps? Not both at the same time, of course! These interdenominational chapels normally carry the main texts of all religions, so it's always possible to get your hands on a Bible, the all-time, global bestseller, and have a good read of the best collection of short stories ever!

Mulling over these short stories in airports – most of them about the ultimate death-journey ahead of us – gives a whole new, realistic, optimistic meaning to travelling!

But now we celebrate that concept of travelling in the broadest sense – of voyaging from one wordly space to another, passing from an earthly to a heavenly life through the third golden chant of rest and pilgrimage, 'In Paradisum'. Within the traditional funeral rite, this song marks that terrribly poignant time just before and as the body embarks on its final, earthly journey from the altar to the tomb. For Emily (who had absolutely no experience of global travelling) this passage was fearfilled, distressing and frightening. I never hear her words on death without imagining them penned after some nightmare she had. In this poem Dollie (Emily's sister Susan) suddenly appears and all is well.

> Dying! Dying in the night!
> Won't somebody bring the light
> So I can see which way to go
> Into the everlasting snow?
>
> And 'Jesus'! Where is Jesus gone?
> They said that Jesus – always came –
> Perhaps he doesn't know the House –
> This way, Jesus, Let him pass!
>
> Somebody run to the great gate
> And see if Dollie's coming! Wait!
> I hear her feet upon the stair!
> Death won't hurt – now Dollie's here!
>
> Emily Dickinson

In stark, reassuring contrast to Emilian death-experience and unease, I sing a trinity of quiet, restful, peaceful songs of repose. 'Lux Aeterna' is simple and brief, but when it comes to 'Ego Sum' I just never want to stop singing! I am right there with Martha as Christ reassures her and quells her fears with these words (John 11:26), and for some reason or other I feel he would have said it twice. So I sing it twice for you! Then, 'In Paradisum' leads us 'with Lazarus and a choir of angels' gently yet firmly on our way to taste some of the best wine yet!

THE
BEST WINE

MARIA

Images of Mary, words and notions associated with her, are complicated because in the twentieth century we have gained new meanings for the femaleness of our being (regardless of whether we are women or men). Notions of Mary often present historical ideas which jostle with each other, throwing us into contradictions and incompatibilities which seem impossible to resolve. What we can do here is simply sing with the music of Mary, allow its healing graces to move us, and to move us along ... let the words come and go in and out of the historical mists; cherish a loose, vague sense of the image of Mary. We can sidestep the philosophical and theological complexities, leaving them to another time, another space, perhaps even to others whose life's work it is to tease out such complexities in an overall theoretical framework. Here, we are in a celebratory mood. Here, marking an achievement or perhaps a journey, singing out our new sense of being, our new sense of being female, through the traditional forms. And why not? The tradition of Mary *must* be big enough to embrace our contemporary sense of femininity, throbbing as it is with hope and possibility and a feeling of strength. And if the words don't yet fit, we'll stretch them ... if the songs are there, we'll sing them!

Images of Mary have inspired so many works of art throughout all times and artistic media. In poetry, my best-loved Marian portrayal is drawn by the nineteenth-century spiritual poet Gerard Manley Hopkins. 'O live air ... worldmothering air, air wild', he calls out to her. The painting of Mary which is 'the apple of my eye' resides in a church in Augsburg, Germany. Though I cannot recall the artist's name, I do recall the title: 'Maria Knotenlöserin', meaning 'Mary, the loosener of knots'. As the Holy Spirit looks on, Mary is totally engrossed in her task of unravelling a long ribbon which has many knots in it. With this image in mind, I imagine our guardian angels all together hovering around as they wait not just for Mary to unravel our earthly knots but for us to allow her to do so!

In music now, here are my Marian chant hits. That symbol of 'the best wine', which is often used of Mary, is so appropriate to sum up the unspeakable richness of the repertoire of Gregorian Chant dedicated to Mary. The term is borrowed from the precious vignette in St John's Gospel, at what is one of the finest moments in the Gospel, John's own diary of the wedding feast at Cana. This is one of the very few times when Mary actually speaks in the Gospels, and she gently but firmly nudges Jesus into action, to throw him out of the nest into his first miracle! A marvellous, miraculous story, which ends with the unsuspecting waiter accusing the groom of 'keeping the best wine' until last. By the way, the best *Gospel* wine for me is this particular Gospel by John, the apostle and son of Zebedee. It also comes last in the New Testament and was written last too, I think. In just forty pages, every conceivable emotion is visited and revisited, leaving you exhilarated. You know you've been through something – a once-off experience, that feeling when you're back at the bottom of the mountain you've just climbed!

Salve Mater Misericordiæ

Chorus

S

al-ve ma-ter mi-se-ri-cór-di-æ, Ma-ter De-i, et ma-ter

vé-ni-æ, Ma-ter spe-i et ma-ter grá-ti-æ,

Ma-ter ple-na sanc-tæ læ-tí-ti-æ. O Ma-rí-a!

S

al-ve de- cus humá-ni gé-ne-ris, Sal-ve Virgo

dig-ni-or cé-te-ris, Quæ vir-gi-nes om-nes transgré-de-

ris, et al-ti-us se-des in su-pe-ris. O Ma-rí-a!

SALVE MATER MISERICORDIAE

Created by God's finger, made in God's image,
O Mary, worthy of praise. The sky is aglow,
the elements receive the joys of life.
It is of you they sing!

Cum Processit – Antiphon
Hildegard Von Bingen (1098-1179)

CHORUS:

Salve mater misericórdiae,
Mater Dei, et mater
véniae,
Mater spei et mater grátiae,
Mater plena sanctae laetítiae.
O Mária!

Salve decus humáni géneris,
Salve Virgo dígnior céteris,
Quae virgines omnes
transgréderis,
et altius sedes in superis.
O María!
CHORUS

Salve félix Virgo puérpera:
Nam qui sédet in Pátris
déxtera,
Caelum régens, terram et
aéthera,
Intra túa se clausit víscera.
O María!
CHORUS

We greet you,
Mother of mercy,
Mother of God, and mother
of forgiveness, Mother of
hope and mother of grace,
Mother filled with holy joy.
O Mary! Hail, honour of the
human race, Hail, Virgin
worthy above all others, You
surpass all virgins and you are
seated on high above them.
O Mary! Hail, happy virgin,
who gave birth to Him who
sits at the Father's right hand,
King of heaven, earth and
sky, He enclosed himself in
your womb. O Mary!

MEDITATION

Here is my perfect scale of eight Marian hymns of praise – of her motherhood, her joy, her virginity, her queenship, her goddess qualities, and above all her powers of healing, peacemaking and justice, which our world today so critically cries out for.

'Salve Mater' is a romantic, sentimental Marian hymn which has a modern ring to it. The maudlin side of my musical nature is forever harmonising the two tailpieces: 'O Maria!' Even as I write, the harmonies are dancing in my soul!

Talking of harmony, the legendary folk singer Pete Seeger, from the Hudson Bay area, is often quoted as saying: 'Singing in harmony is singing any note your neighbour isn't!' So in that unbridled Seegerian spirit, harmonise away! That same unbridled spirit is released for me in singing this chant over an open fifth drone of C–G.

A further note on the sound notes you hear now. Over the forty chants, some which I sing solo, some with 'the lads' (my term of endearment for the St Patrick's student priests), I've kept before me the reality that you might be looking at the printed music of the chants, following my every note on paper. This reality was a great shock to my musical system at first because I just love, and cannot help, playing around with the sounds and notes, making my own of them. This is very different from any other recording I've made before – and it's a process I'm ultimately uneasy with because there's just nothing to compare with the live performance, as we call it. Singing comes a-live in the live situation. All the elements of life are there: you, as singer, are interacting with others; they're responding, co-creators of the sound, and together we're shaping the space I often refer to, where 'God comes to us and we go to God'. That chant space we're trying to reach right now. However, in the absence of that live contact, technology is quite literally a God-send! All of this is simply to say that I got carried away just once or twice and the odd *sean-nós* influence or two crept in through the cracks of passion and devotion! Add your own personal, wayward touches too!

Ave Maria

Of all women you are the most blessed, and blessed
is the fruit of your womb.

Luke 1:42

Ave María, grátia
plena, Dóminus
tecum, benedícta tu in
muliéribus, et benedíctus
fructus ventris tui, Jesus.

Sancta María, Mater Dei, ora
pro nobis peccatóribus
nunc et in hora mortis
nostrae. Amen.

Hail Mary, full of
grace, the Lord is
with thee, blessed art thou
among women and blessed is
the fruit of thy womb, Jesus.
Holy Mary, Mother of God,
pray for us sinners, now and
at the hour of our death.
Amen.

<dt>25</dt>

MEDITATION

As children, out of adult earshot and in defiance and unconscious rejection of enforced inheritance, we brazenly and joyfully canted:

> Hail Mary, full of grace,
> The cat fell down and broke his face.
> Holy Mary, mother of God,
> If I was your mother, I'd give you the rod!

Later, a new meaning to the 'Hail Mary' began, the start of a real relationship which is alive and well today, when I, like everyone else in my school year, became a Child of Mary. The rather drab school uniform was transformed into the most regal gown every morning as I ritualistically pinned on my Child of Mary medal on the right-hand side, just above the breast-pocket! No more cursing, no more lies, no more whistling! Mary doesn't like it when you curse, tell lies or whistle, and she'll cry!

'Hail Mary' in song throws light in two memory directions: the first musical setting of the 'Ave Maria' which I heard and sang was the sentimental composition of Charles Gounod. I met it in formal singing lessons when I was ten, and have sung it at many a wedding and ordination since! I only knew it then as *Gunó's* 'Ave Maria' and as far as I was aware or cared, Charles Gounod could have been a *sean-nós* singer from Kerry! But this nineteenth-century French composer followed me through my college days. A colourful character he appears to have been, more on the dark side and not very popular it seems, from the many anecdotes and stories that live on in his name. This was a real eye-opener to me because I had always believed – and still do – from my own one-to-one experience of musicians, that people living with music are among the greatest, finest, nicest people in the world! But the story goes that on one occasion when the pianist Charles Hallé played in Paris, Gounod went to enormous lengths to praise Hallé's performance, reliving many moments of the Beethoven sonata which he had just played. Next thing, Gounod's unsuspecting wife came up and apologised for their having missed the recital due to a prior commitment! Or the story of the most popular opera of the time, Gounod's *Faust*. This caused great controversy in the 1920s when it was brought to light that Gounod had some fifty years before stolen a score – presumably of the *Faust* music – from a young composer who had died in an asylum. I'll leave Charles Gounod with his own rather arrogant, priggish comment when some poor innocent woman asked how he composed his melodies. 'Madame,' he said, 'God sends down some of his angels and they whisper sweet melodies in my ear.'

The second memory flashes back to the beginning of my second-level school spell. At the age of thirteen, this plainchant antiphon we sing here was to course through my blood for the first time, and for thirty-odd years now it has flowed faster and freer than Gounod's nostalgic air ever could! The melody has a life all of its own, taking one's soul and imagination into the realms of the spirit. Sometimes, singing this air, you think suddenly that you've gone astray! But why not? As we say in Irish: Sure, didn't you see more of the country because of it!

Just look and listen to the musical setting of this most famous name: Maria. We meet it twice here, and both times it rightly heralds the highest note of each of the two parts of this prayer, the first Maria introducing the note C, the second soaring off up to high D! I never hear this name Maria without summoning up the poignant phrase from Bernstein's *West Side Story* – 'Maria! I just met a girl name Maria!'

Now, I was christened Nora Mary Antoinette: Nora, because my mother and grandmother were also Nora – and I was 'little Nora', so Nóirín is the diminutive form, although there's nothing little about me now! The Antoinette tag celebrated the day after I was born – June 13th – which is the feastday of St Anthony (yes, the saint I mentioned to whom we prayed when we lost the hold of ourselves or of anything else! The right man for me to be entrusted to!) But the Mary name was just given to me – 'No rhyme or reason why', my mother tells me. 'Sure, everyone was called after Mary then,' she replied when I questioned her one time. And that was indeed the case in Ireland up to recently: all female religious were also called Mary – Sr Mary Paschal, Sr Mary Rumold and so on; men as well as women were given Mary as a second name. The man who springs to mind now, and God knows how happy he or any other man was to carry that name on his back, is Joseph Mary Plunkett! A Dublinman, he was executed for his part in the 1916 rising at the age of thirty-one. 'For many live that one may die / And one must die that many live', he wrote of Christ's death on the cross; apocalyptic lines, revealing his own destiny.

Hildegard Von Bingen, the Benedictine abbess who lived eight hundred years ago, prayed and sang: *O suavis Virgo, in te non deficit ullum gaudium* (Sweet Virgin, there is no shortage of joy in you). Hildegard earns her true seat of tribute here because of all the spiritual songs which she composed, the vast majority of them were inspired by Mary. At the age of forty-two and seven months (that seven cycle again!) she began, for the first time, to record her extraordinary stories, visions, scientific and medical treatises, her ecological and cosmological insights. Her all-pervasive creativity she described as: 'writing, seeing, hearing and knowing all in one manner'. This resonates with Emily Dickinson's description of true poetry: 'If I feel physically as if the top of my head were taken off, I know that is poetry.' But timing again dictates the re-birth of everything Hildegardian, and now, in the midst of twentieth-century global and ecclesiastical crisis, her comet shines brightly in the sky!

The first-known woman composer in Western history, her cast of chant stands out firmly in its own boat in the seas of Gregorian Chant, breaking all the rules and boundaries to prove that praying is for everyone and everyone has a stamp of their own! An older Gregorian Chant scholar once defined Hildegard's chant for me as 'The eroticisation of Gregorian Chant'. Nothing wrong with that! Whatever about eros, Hildegard's song is full of unadulterated, wholesome joy, and to sing it is a pure tonic! But it's much, much more too. The many hours I've spent making my own, on my own, of Hildegard's songs have rewarded me a hundredfold. But one sharing of Hildegardian chant stands out above them all.

RTÉ, our broadcasting station, once asked me to present Vespers on radio from the only Irish female Benedictine monastery, Kylemore Abbey, situated in the midst of the otherworldly landscape of Connemara. I was full of Hildegard at the time and it seemed so logical and providential to call on her to celebrate with this Benedictine women's community. So once a week for the few weeks beforehand, I would set out in the early morning from home, drop my children for the day, and don the hat of the Hildegard fan and teacher. As I drove across the Inagh valley just minutes before arriving, it always seemed as if the mountains above me, reflected in the lakes below me, were God's stepping stones – a sacred bridge between my domestic world and the world of this praying community of women of the black cloth! Just the right spiritual initiation rite! Six singing sisters worked hard and the musical and spiritual mission was gladsomely accomplished!

However, for me the experience was particularly memorable for launching a daily ritual since then. The wise elder in the midst of our *schola* was a wonderful Limerick woman, Sister Gregory. In her eighties then, she sang with a honeyed voice, as true and as heavenly as any I've heard before or since. One evening, as I sat alone with her, I shared my enthusiasm for and appreciation of her singing. Had she any secret? How did she do it, I asked. She threw her head back and laughed. 'I think it could be that every morning when I get out of bed for morning office, I stand in front of my open window, say a prayer of thanksgiving and take three deep breaths of God's air,' she said. I think so, too, dear Sister Gregory, and often think of you as I too breathe that same godly air today. You chose the right name too as a singer of Gregorian Chant for most of your life, and may you sing out a daily prayer for us now in God's company!

Concordi Lætitia

Con-cór-di læ-tí-ti-a, Pro-púl-sa mœs-tí-ti-a,

Ma-rí-æ præ-có-ni-a Ré-co-lat Ec-clé-si-a;

Vir-go Ma-rí-a!

Fair fragrant seat chosen by the King,
The noble guest who was in your womb three times
three months.

Prayer to the Virgin, St Colm Cille (d.597)

Concórdi laetítia,
Propúlsa maestítia,
Maríae praecónia
Récolat Ecclésia;
    Virgo María!

Quam concéntu párali
Chori laudant caelici,
Et nos cum caeléstibus,
Novem melos pángimus;
    Virgo María!

Gloriósa Trínitas,
Indivísa Unitas,
Ob Maríae mérita,
Nos salva per saecula;
    Virgo María!

United in joy, hating sorrow, Mary's proclamation renews the church. O Virgin Mary! Choirs of heaven, joined in harmony, sing praise, and we, with the heavenly ones, sing a new song. O Virgin Mary! Glorious Trinity, undivided Unity, Through Mary's merits, save us forever. O Virgin Mary!

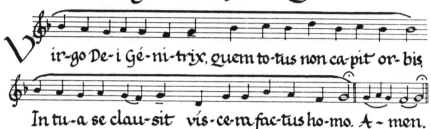

Noble the being born from you,
you were granted, Mary, a great gift:
Christ, son of God, the Father in heaven,
him have you borne in Bethlehem.

Blathmac (c. 750)

Virgo Dei Génitrix,
    quem totus non capit
orbis
in tua se clausit víscera factus
    homo.

Véra fídes gémiti, purgávit
    crímina múndi.
et tíbi virgínitas invioláta
    mánet.

Te mátrem pietátis, opem te
    clámitat órbis,
subvénias fámulis, o
    benedícta, túis. Amen.

Virgin Mother of God,
    He whom the whole
world cannot contain
enclosed himself in your
womb and was made man.
Truly in faith you gave birth
to the one who cleanses the
sins of the world and you
remain truly a virgin. To you,
mother of compassion, the
world cries for help, you
come O Blessed one to help
your family. Amen.

O Pia Virgo

Mary beloved! Mother of the White Lamb,
Shield, o shield us, pure Virgin of nobleness.

Hymn of the Beltane Procession, Scotland

CHORUS:

O pia Virgo, Mater et alma,
Nostra benígne, Súscipe vota.

Sancta María, Te decus omne
Caélitus ornat, Teque
supérna, Grátia replet.
CHORUS.

Casta colúmba, Advenis orbi
Núntia vitae, Pacis in ore
Pígnora portans.
CHORUS.

Spléndida stella, Per maris
undas
Ne pereámus, Fulget amíca
Lux tua ductrix.
CHORUS.

Nostra dat intus Vita timóres:
Cúrrimus ad te: Nunc et in
hora Mortis adésto.
CHORUS.

O Blessed Virgin and gentle mother, in your goodness hear our prayers. Holy Mary, all heaven praises you who are full of grace. As the dove that bore the symbol of peace, you come to us with tidings of life. Radiant star of the sea, let your kindly light guide us lest we perish. To you we hasten in the troubles of life: assist us now and at the hour of death.

MEDITATION

Now these three chants differ, but I think of them together. There's an earthy, organic feel from singing and listening to them, a simplicity, almost a plainness to them. As I browsed through the Bible waiting for the right little blessing to present itself for these songs – as they did for all the other thirty-six chants – none seemed to fit. But blessings from the Celtic tradition sat perfectly for me on their shoulders. Firstly, 'Concordi' is blessed by St Colm Cille, founder of Hy, the island of Iona, hymn writer and no doubt chant singer whose memory we toast this year (1997), fourteen hundred years after his death in AD 597. Then Blathmac, an eighth-century poet from County Monaghan has his say. A seventeenth-century manuscript preserved a biblical narrative of over two hundred stanzas of his on the passion of Christ and the sorrows of Mary, and four lines from it addressing Mary launch 'Virgo Dei Genetrix'. Finally, the restrained 'O Pia Virgo' is observed and honoured through an invocation of a traditional Hebridean Mayday hymn of protection.

Straightforwardness and lack of adornment serve to heighten this trio. Firstly the delicate play or dance between rhythm and seeming non-rhythm marks 'Concordi Laetitia'. The verse or main body of the chant is metrical and sings itself in a tender rhythm. Then 'Virgo Maria' assumes its own pace and time, allowing itself to be moulded by the whim of the singer! I sandwiched 'Virgo Dei' between two gems because musically it plods a little. Of four phrases, two are repeated but the pearl of the piece sparkles through the low note in the final phrase. 'Virgo Dei' is the plain one which sets off the others! A friend of mine tells of her grandmother, an avid gardener who carefully adorned her little patch with kaleidoscopic and vivid-coloured flowers. In one tiny nook, she deliberately allowed the dandelions to flourish and thrive. 'Sure, they only set off the rest,' she would always say!

'O Pia Virgo' is always a workshop favourite, with its graceful balance between verse and chorus. The chorus has four phraselets, the verse five – this balance of odd and even again, which is the very quick of humanity!

Regina Cœli

Re - gí - na cœ - li, lœ - tá - re, al- le - lú - ia:

Qui- a quem me- ru- ís- ti por- tá- re, al- le- lú- ia:

Re -sur- ré - xit si - cut di - xit, al- le - lú - ia :

O - ra pro no - bis De - um, al- le - lú - ia.

The queen of Sheba said to Solomon:
Blessed be Yahweh your God who has granted you
his favour, setting you on the throne of Israel.

1 Kings. 10:9

Regína caeli laetáre,
allelúia:
Quia quem meruísti portáre,
allelúia:
Resurréxit sicut dixit,
allelúia:
Ora pro nobis Deum,
allelúia.

Queen of heaven
rejoice, alleluia: He
whom it was your honour to
bear, alleluia: Has risen as
He said, alleluia: Pray for us
to God, alleluia.

MEDITATION

It seemed right that 'the lads' sing the simple 'Regina Caeli' with me here and that it be their final note as it is at Compline, the final prayer-call of each day. Mary always has the last prayer at eventide, another vindication for the last batch of chants here centring on her.

On a personal note, I have had many, many experiences of the power or universality of chant through this extremely well known chant within the Gregorian repertoire. The most dramatic was when I had the unique privilege of introducing His Holiness, the 14th Dalai Lama in song at an international interfaith conference in Costa Rica in 1989. In an enormous cathedral in Carthago, a village outside San José, my brief was to lead His Holiness and the other participants right through the cathedral at the beginning and end of the service.

To the right of the altar in an enclosed space behind a grid barrier were over two hundred young seminarians. They sang some Gregorian Chant beautifully, and at the very end of the ceremony we really wanted to communicate with one another, but I did not speak their Spanish language. So, in frustration, I boldly walked up to the grid that separated us and self-assuredly intoned 'Regina Caeli'. By *laetare*, we were all, quite literally, rejoicing in amalgamated sound, bound together in shared experience. Who needed words – we needed to say no more! The physical grid between us dissolved. Bells in the cathedral added a layer of music and a joyful sound that pealed out over the rainforest, and continued their hymn of praise long after we had ceased. And outside in the brilliant, balmy sunshine of this natural oasis, we were dazzled not just by the awsomeness of what had happened, but by the sights and sounds around us. The music about our ears, the blast of the bells in the belfry were matched by the dancing and swaying of the rainforest trees, which moved in time to the music, never out of step or out of tune, in perfect harmony – the harmony of the cosmos. We stood there for one of those rare occasions when time stands still, soaked in the beauty of creation and its creator. Then these same bells tolled the 'Angelus' at six o clock, even though on that particular evening there was no need to remind us, as the radio announcer here in Ireland does, to 'pause for prayer'.

So 'Regina Caeli' has become an 'Angelus' prayer for me. Since I always found it impossible to remember the quirky, sixteenth-century sequence of prayers that traditionally accompanies this bell-toll, I sometimes just toll 'Regina Caeli' from the belfry of my heart.

In Ireland the 'Angelus' bell still punctuates the daytime of many villagers. It did mine, every day at noon and 6pm, up to three years ago. Then we moved from the village-centre to three miles down the road where we rebuilt the family nest for the third time! Hindu tradition allows you three goes. By the third time round, you should have got the hang of it! We feel that this is true for us in Dromore and every day I sing and pray that God will be with us here as long as we are! But I do feel the loss of that minareted call to prayer which drew us, inadvertently, into a solid praying community. It seemed to me to be a momentary adjournment when in the silence between the chimes, a messenger passed by and touched our lips. So, six o'clock in the evening, honouring Carthago and the rainforest, and the angels, messengers of life and death, sees me turn on the television when the screen freezes on some icon or artistic representation of the 'Angelus' story for half a minute. Through this chant, with an overture of Sign of the Cross, I try to admit in whatever tidings God, Mary and the cosmos have for me. It is my wish and prayer that you will also sing along through the 'Regina Caeli' because I genuinely feel that it contains a secret formula of emotional renewal and elation that is accessible to us all, singers and listeners alike.

AveMaris Stella

And it is said, the Virgin's names was Mary,
which translated means – 'Star of the Sea'.

St Bernard of Clairvaux (1090-1153)

Ave maris stella,
Dei Mater alma,
Atque semper Virgo,
Felix caeli porta.

Sumens illud Ave
Gabriélis ore,
Funda nos in pace,
Mutans Hevae nomen.

Vitam praesta puram,
Iter para tutum:
Ut, vidéntes Jesum,
Semper collaetémur.

Sit laus Deo Patri,
Summo Christo decus,
Spíritui Sancto,
Tribus honor unus. Amen.

Hail star of the sea,
God's loving mother,
always a virgin, heaven's fair
gate. You who received that
'hail' from Gabriel's lips,
create us in peace, reversing
the name 'Eva'. Make it your
care that our life is sinless,
prepare a safe journey for us
so that we may see Jesus and
rejoice together for ever. May
praise be to God the Father,
to Christ the most high, to
the Holy Spirit, to the three
be equal honour. Amen.

MEDITATION

For every one of the many images and thoughts buzzing in my head to share with you on paper, there will be at least three more that time will run out on. So bear with me a little longer! Now you know my style, I'll leave it to you to flesh out the bare bones, to clothe the skeletal thought, to let your *own* imagination fly! And from that same prayer mat of humility I feel also a confidence that if I can find the spirit here, then so can you; if I can sing that sacred song, say that sacred word, so you can and must do for yourself, for God and the universe – and for all the world to hear!

Look and listen now to 'Ave Maris Stella'. The few tangible facts I know for you: a seventh- or eighth-century prayer, six syllables to every line, this jaunty little tune was recycled by an Irish priest in 1916. Fr Pádraig Breathnach published a collection of twenty-four hymns in Irish called *Raint Amhrán*. What is presumably his own hymn of praise to Brighid (the Irish spelling for Brigid, pronounced Breathe), he chose to set to this tune. What matters to my heart every time I sing this chant is this Brighid connection. For me it is a siamese-twin chant, one verse sings to Mary, the next to the goddess (later saint) Brighid.

The goddess Brighid – triple goddess and matron of healing, poetry and smithscraft – taps into the pagan and pre-Christian roots that are, thankfully, still part and parcel of each one of us. The historical Brighid, Christian saint, was born in Ireland about AD 457, but her influence is not confined to her homeland alone. Legend has it that the medieval knights of chivalry chose Brighid as their patroness, and it was they who first called their wives 'brides'.

Four toasts to Brigid now. My first toast I call 'The Singing Flame'. Apparently in all Brigidine convents from the fifth to the fifteenth centuries, according to her wishes, a flame was kept alive to symbolise hospitality, warmth, growth and light. In 1993, the Brigidine sisters of Ireland rekindled this flame in Kildare, and I will always cherish the time then, and many times since, that I have enveloped that original flame in song and chant. Brigid herself it was, I'm sure, who manipulated one particular meeting I had with these wonderful, fiery sisters on an evening in June, two years ago now. As I was giving the customary run-down of my travel diary to them, the highlight was an upcoming visit to China to sing at the Fourth United Nations Women's Conference in Beijing. We all hit on it together! Would I – could I – carry the flame? What a symbol of ongoing female strength and spirituality! The anwer to the first half was the most positive 'Yes' of my life. But how could I carry a naked flame, a burning candle, half-way across the world? An ingenious plan was devised and executed by the inventive, competent Gay Brabazon and Sisters Mary and Phil. I carried the flame on board the plane in a charcaol handwarmer which lasted eight hours until I got to Moscow; I then rekindled from this stick another which lasted right into China! All I can say here, friends, in the light of my experiences of carrying Brigid's light is that she's a trickster and loved 'kicking her heels' in style from the Curragh to the Great Wall! So here's to Brigid of the singing flame!

The second toast has all got to do with timing again. The first two days of February had special significance to our pagan Celtic forebears. February the first was the great spring festival called Imbolg, and February the second was the time of light when candles and torches were boldly carried through the countryside at night, dispelling the darkness and evil which could befall at any time. Christianisation in the West is like a hermit crab, that small soft-bodied crustacean living in and carrying about the empty shells of bygone whelks – it superimposed itself cleverly on paganism, and on these two spring days. Celebration of nature and light still lives on, now in a different form.

Brigid – goddess and now Christian saint – our *Muire na nGael* (Mary of the Irish), heralds not just the first day in February but the first day of our spring. February the second honours the purity and holiness of the other Mary – *Muire na ndaoine* (Mary of the people) – but candles and many forms of light are the symbol of the day which is called both 'the Presentation' and 'Candlemas'. At Glenstal Abbey, celebration of the daily community mass on this day begins at the bottom of the church with the monks and the few of us gathered there holding our blessed lighted candles and singing: *Lumen ad revelationem gentium* (a light revealed to the people). For that split-second we are coursing through all the belief systems – pagan and Christian – of our ancestors. The candle I hold every year at Candlemass is then carefully stored away to be taken out, rekindled, prayed and sung beside, at the many difficult times over the coming year when darkness of any kind looms large. And it always does the dispelling trick!

February the third heralds the feast of the patron of singers, St Blaise, and here again Brigid sings her healing song. Traditionally in Ireland, a piece of cotton cloth (*brat* as it is called in Irish) was left outside the door on the last night of January in the belief that Brigid would bless the cloth as she passed by. Any painful throat in the household during the year would vanish once the cloth touched it. I never go anywhere without my *brat Bhríde*! Here's to Brigid, the healer with the cloth!

The third toast takes the form of a legend from our Irish tradition. It celebrates and situates these two Christian feastdays with a delicate hint of myth and mystery, which captures the imagination and spiritual mix of what we have inherited – a Celtic Christianity which is both literal and symbolic, all at the one time. Mary and Jesus are making their way to Jerusalem. Soldiers appear before them, preventing the two from completing their journey. In despair Mary calls on Brigid to assist her. Enter Brigid, who has enveloped her head with a crown of lighting candles. Of course, the soldiers are enchanted, and during their distraction, Mary and her little one pass by unnoticed. 'Thank you, Brigid,' Mary calls back to her. 'From this day onwards, your feastday will always be before mine.' Here's to Brigid the ingenious!

My final Brigidine toast, in this quartet of tributes to the spirit of a triple goddess, is a little Brigidian chant in its own way. I can hear her singing her song which is chock-full of simple, unalloyed joys of flesh and spirit! Brigid's definition of pure prayer here has brought healing and holy smiles to many people I've performed to throughout the four corners of the earth and I hope it does to you now! Her own words, which you see below, from an 1861 manuscript, are in Old Irish and are translated and enhanced through the uplifting hand of poet Brendan Kennelly.

> I'd like to give a lake of beer to God.
> > I'd love the Heavenly
> Host to be tippling there
> > For all eternity.
>
> I'd love the men of Heaven to live with me,
> > To dance and sing.
> If they wanted, I'd put at their disposal
> > Vats of suffering.
>
> White cups of love I'd give them
> > With a heart and a half;
> Sweet pitchers of mercy I'd offer
> > To every man.

I'd make Heaven a cheerful spot
    Because the happy heart is true.
I'd make the men contented for their own sake.
    I'd like Jesus to love me too.

I'd like the people of Heaven to gather
    From all the parishes around.
I'd give a special welcome to the women,
    The three Marys of great renown.

I'd sit with the men, the women of God
    There by the lake of beer.
We'd be drinking good health forever
    And every drop would be a prayer.
Brendan Kennelly

We're singing good health for ever – and every note is a prayer! Good health, happy hearts, true contentment, dancing, minds drunk with praises of God and one another, cheerfulness, peace and singing – the elixir of life and religion all rolled up Brigid's heaven. Sounds just like my style of heaven!

As I mentioned already, the Irish form of Brigid is Brid or Brighid and is pronounced Breathe, which shares that image of breathing, breath, spirit – the essence of singing and of chant which in Latin is *spiritus*. And just as each breath in our bodies is a once-off, so is this chant. Not just in its maverick personality but because in the recording, along with the 'Magnificat' coming up, I gave it my 'almighty best' for you in a once-off, single shot.

Magnificat cum Alleluia

Antiphon 1

Al - le-lú - ia, al-le-lú - ia, al - le - lu - ia.

Mag~ní ~ fi - cat á-ni-ma me-a Dó-mi-num.

Antiphon 2

Al - le-lú ~ ia, al ~ le ~ lú - ia.

2. Et exsultávit spíritus me ~ us
4. Qui ~ a fe-cit mihi magna qui po ~ tens est:
6. Fe ~ cit poténtiam in bráchio su ~ o:
8. E ~ suriéntes implévit bo ~ nis:
10. Si ~ cut locútus est ad patres nos ~ tros:
12. Si ~ cut erat in princípio, et nunc, et sem ~ per;

2. in De ~ o salu ~ tá-ri me-o.
4. et sanc-tum no-men e-jus.
6. dispérsit su-pér-bos mente cor-dis su-i.
8. et dí - vites dimí ~ sit in-á-nes.
10. Abraham et sé - mini e-jus in sǽcu-la.
12. et in sǽ - cula sæcu- ló-rum. A-men.

Antiphon 1.

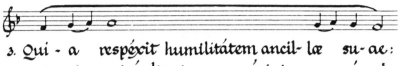

3. Qui - a respéxit humilitátem ancil- læ su - ae:
5. Et mi - sericórdia ejus a progénie in pro - gé - nies
7. De - pó - suit poténtes de se - de,
9. Sus - cé - pit Israel púe - rum su - um,
11. Gló - ri - a Patri, et Fil - i - o,

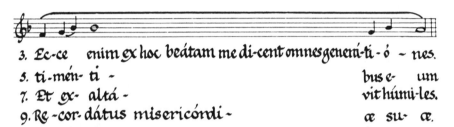

3. Ec-ce enim ex hoc beátam me di-cent omnes generá-ti - ó - nes.
5. ti - mén - ti - bus e - um
7. Et ex - altá - vit húmi-les.
9. Re -cor- dátus misericórdi - æ su - æ.
11. Et Spi -rítu - i Sancto.

Antiphon 2

MAGNIFICAT CUM ALLELUIA

Then Hannah said this prayer:
'My heart exults in Yahweh ...
Do not speak and speak with haughy words,
let not arrogance come from your mouth.

1 Samuel 2:1,2,3

ALLELÚIA, ALLELÚIA, ALLELÚIA.

Magníficat ánima mea Dóminum.
Et exsultávit spíritus meus in Deo salutári meo.
Allelúia, allelúia, allelúia.

Quia respéxit humilitátem ancillae suae: Ecce enim ex hoc beátam me dicent omnes generatiónes.
Allelúia, allelúia.

Quia fecit mihi magna qui potens est: et sanctum nomen ejus.
Allelúia, allelúia, allelúia.

Et misericórdia ejus a progénie in progénies timentibus eum.
Allelúia, allelúia.

Fecit poténtiam in bráchio suo: dispérsit supérbos mente cordis sui.
Allelúia, allelúia, allelúia.

My soul proclaims the greatness of the Lord. My spirit rejoices in God my saviour. For he has looked upon his servant in her lowliness: all ages to come will call me blessed. God the Almighty has done great things for me: and holy is His name. His mercy is from age to age on those who fear Him. He has shown the might of His arm: He has confused the proud in their deepest thoughts. He has deposed the mighty from their thrones and raised the lowly to high places. The hungry He has given every good thing: while the rich He has sent empty away. He has upheld Israel His servant,

Depósuit poténtes de sede, et
  exaltávit húmiles.
Allelúia, allelúia.

Esuriéntes implévit bonis: et
  dívites dimísit inánes.
Allelúia, allelúia, allelúia.

Suscépit Israel púerum suum
  recordátus misericórdiae
  suae.
Allelúia, allelúia.

Sicut locútus est ad patres
  nostros: Abraham et
  sémini ejus in saécula.
Allelúia, allelúia, allelúia.

Glória Patri, et Fílio, et
  Spirítui Sancto.
Allelúia, allelúia.

Sicut erat in princípio, et
  nunc, et semper, et in
  saécula saeculórum.
  Amen.
Allelúia, allelúia, allelúia.
Allelúia, allelúia, allelúia.

ever mindful of His mercy.
As He promised our fathers,
Abraham and his
descendants forever. Glory be
to the Father, Son and Holy
Spirit, as it was in the
beginning is now and ever
shall be world without end.
Amen.

MEDITATION

Ten principles of justice, fairness, peace which have passed the lips of our foreparents for at least three thousand, two hundred years are here before you! The oldest song in the overall book of Christian chant and the second last song in this book! Oldest because even though the 'Magnificat' text here is taken straight from St Luke's Gospel, an almost exact replica appears in the first book of Samuel in the historical books of the Old Testament, written hundreds of years earlier. Here Hannah, mother of Samuel, presents her young son to the Lord, singing the original 'Magnificat': 'My heart exults in the Lord, my horn is exalted in my God, my mouth derides my foes, for I rejoice in your power of saving. He raises the poor from the dust, he lifts the needy from the dunghill to give them a place with princes. He safeguards the steps of his faithful but the wicked vanish in darkness.'(I Samuel 2:1-10) Hannah's song must have inspired Luke, even with regard to structure, since both songs – the Old Testament and New Testament versions – fall into ten verses.

Now, I'm no Biblical scholar. Indeed, maybe I'm only speaking for myself, but as a Roman Catholic child I was never taught to navigate the Biblical seas thoroughly or with enthusiasm, particularly these Old Testament seas. When I got around to sailing these seas, I found it a handful! A handful in the best sense of the word because it threw up for me a handful of five mighty women, one for every finger! Of these five, three have entire books dedicated to their memory – the Books of Ruth, Judith and Esther. Ruth's story – the eighth book of the Pentateuch – is a gem of a story of love and loyalty. A non-Israelite, Ruth, because of her piety and integrity, was favoured by God and joined to the Israelites through marriage. Esther was a fifth-century BC queen of Persia who averted a pogrom against her people, saving them from annihilation.

My hat comes off to Judith! A wild woman by all accounts, she must have had a streak of Irish blood in her somewhere! Judith, having single-handedly cut off the head of Holofernes, the general in charge of the Assyrian army who lay on his bed 'sodden with wine' which she herself encouraged him to consume, later harnessed her mules, hitched her wagons to them and loaded up all his 'silver, his couches, his dishes and all his furniture' (Judith 15:11). It seems so appropriate as I sing this salvation song of sheer lustiness and power to take up the legend of Judith from the end of Chapter 15, painting, first-hand, the remaining colourful canvas of feminine revelry, praise and thanksgiving on that day over two thousand years ago. Because we're all singing the same song really and some things from the heart never change.

'All the women of Israel gathered to see her; and they blessed her and performed a dance in her honour. She took branches in her hands and distributed them to the women around her and she and the other women crowned themselves with garlands of olive leaves. At the head of all the people she led the women in the dance, while the men followed in their armour wearing garlands and singing hymns. Judith led all Israel in this song of thanksgiving ... "a song to my God with timbrels, chant to the Lord with cymbals; Sing a new song."' No wonder she lived to the age of one hundred and five!

The fourth great woman is Miriam. In fact, the first mention of women and singing in the Hebrew Bible, the Old Testament, I think rests on her. Just imagine her exuberance having witnessed the miracle of the Red Sea, or the Sea of Reeds, when her people had just walked on dry ground through the sea, free from the clutches of Pharaoh. Her song of thanksgiving is history! Miriam, the prophetess, Aaron's sister, along with all the other women, playing their tambourines, dancing and singing: 'Sing of the Lord: he has covered himself in glory, horse and rider he has thrown into the sea' (Exodus 15:21).

The fifth member of this handful is the other Israelite prophetess and judge Deborah, whom we meet in the Book of Judges. A wise woman, she 'used to sit under Deborah's Palm between Ramah and Bethel in the highlands of Ephraim, and the Israelites would come to her to have their disputes decided'. This fifth heroine in the fifth chapter of Judges sings her own 'Magnificat' for all the world to sing and hear.

Now the circle of reconnection back to that role of prophecy and equality in God is complete. In our common search for and exploration of finding new ways of going halves to God, one constant remains in the midst. And that contemporary common ground is Gregorian Chant where so much imagery and language spans all ages, all genders, all theologies of Old and New Testaments, old and new spiritualities, old and new people.

But this magnificent 'Magnificat cum Alleluia' is my theme song and I very deliberately sing it now at this exact finishing point in the aural and visual timespace we share. No day passes without my airing it: either when I attend Vespers in Glenstal where around 6.40pm we pray it quietly and unostentatiously through one of the eight Gregorian Chant tones; or when I sing it alone at some time in the day, here in the kitchen, with the surpeti as you hear it now; or it darts in and out – in bits and pieces, here, there, anywhere – visiting my mind like the swift evening starlings in the outhouses! Corresponding to these starlings in flight, the 'Magnificat' in flight for me is this version where every lofty, noble impression is constantly heightened and interrupted by the greatest cry of jubilation: Alleluia! Every Alleluia becomes a starling singing in God's garden!

GO
IN PEACE

Da Pacem Domine

D a pa-cem Dó-mi-ne in di - é - bus nos-tris:

qui-a non est á-li-us

Qui pug-net pro no-bis, ni-si tu De-us nos-ter.

Da pacem Dómine in diébus nostris: quia non est álius qui pugnet pro nobis, nisi tu Deus noster.

Grant us peace, O Lord in our day: for no one else will fight for us except you, our God.

MEDITATION

A landscape can sing about God, a body about Spirit.

Dag Hammarskjöld

From this body's song about spirit, ranging from truth and beauty to sadness and mirth, here is the final note, the vocal, verbal and actual full stop – well, two full stops! I simply could not resist singing this peace-chant twice for you. And just look at the little flourish of six notes on *alius*, in the inspired tradition of chant, as we turn our gaze here towards God in a final plea for protection.

POST-MEDITATION

And wisdom is a butterfly
William Butler Yeats

For me, Gregorian Chant is the most colourful reverberating butterfly of any time, of any place. I've been trying to resound for you, in sound, sight and story, its elusiveness, its unpredictability, its soul – all of which are indefinable in many ways, like trying to describe prayer or meditation. So the adage borrowed from Lao Tzu of sixth-century China, 'The way to do is to be', still sings true. In weaving the threads of 'doing' and 'being' in the making of this spiritual chantbag, just three mental saddle-stitches remain and the work is done!

The first finishing stitch has all that elusiveness and fleeting butterfly features. It is about the most sacred moment of space between sound and silence – the moment just before the first note of a chant is sounded. This actual second before birthing a note, birthing that chant within your head, is vocal dreamtime. A vocal *altjeringa* – borrowing now from the Australian Aboriginal tradition – where we dream the sound into being. A God-given process, primal and ritualistic.

'And deep things are song', wrote the Scottish essayist and historian Thomas Carlyle (1795-1881). And deep things are chants, too. And is that butterfly-song that's flying round and round in the head ready to be born? Will that first note of the chant be there? Where does it come from? In the Overture, Sinéad and I talk of the voice between the heart and the head. Through singing chant, that same voice now shimmers in the infinite space between heaven and earth – the body earthing these heavenly songs to bring us all to our destiny: 'establishing', 'making fast and firm' our souls in the truest sense of the original meaning of the Latin word, *destinare*.

The second-last stitch loops in and out of a truly inspired story from the Talmud, the great encyclopaedia of Jewish teaching.

> In that unknown twilight before a child is born, a bright light is held behind its head which illuminates the whole world, from one end to the other. All knowledge and wisdom is endowed through this sight and the entire Torah – the whole body of Jewish sacred writings – is then imbibed into this soul. At the very moment of birth, an angel touches the child on the lips. All the acquired wisdom is forgotten then and the whole of one's life is spent remembering what was once known.

Amidst a mound of my personal soul-notes, this tale appears with no birth certificate and as if an angel touched this story on the lips, all memory of source and history is forgotten! The legend is itself some kind of timeless chant and has an unknown yet familiar corresponding gamut of sound-notes. Reading between the lines, between the words, I can always see this tale finely etched on a plainchant manuscript, with snatches of many of these forty melodies which we've shared, playfully fading in and out. Listening between the notes of Gregorian Chant *is* a hint of that forgotten wisdom, a taste of what was once known before some angel, very close to us now, touched our lips. That same angel brings echoes of the original message through these spiritual melodies, touching our lips and stirring that memory in me, in you, because –

> Blossoms will run away,
> Cakes reign but a Day,
> But memory like Melody
> Is pink Eternally.
>
> Emily Dickinson

And the final stitch-thought stems from two inexhaustible wells which inspired me throughout: certainty and truth – two words which in Greek and Hebrew appropriately mean *amen*! My staunch belief in the certainty of the belief-system, the words, the music, the sharing, the memory, the ultimate meaning of it all which Gregorian Chant embodies today. And truth in drafting my own personal Gregorian Chant story, which in its occasional eccentricities, impulses and whims is, in a way, a 'Stubborn cleaving to the timbre, the tones of what we are, Even when all the texts describe it differently' (Adrienne Rich).

From that celestial tome, the great elysian book of Gregorian Chant, I have browsed through the Index and selected just forty song-chapters that whispered and sang to my heart. But now, it's time to move on, to let go, to reverently and quietly replace the volume on the shelves of heavenly time. It's time also to fade down the volume of our singing – our honest 'kernels of sound' and, just once more, to leave you peacefully in the palm of poetry's hand, a finale which completes the divine cycle of past, present and future.

> Certain kernels of sound
> reverberate like seasoned timber,
> unmuted truths of a people's winters.
> stirrings of a thousand different
> springs.
>
> Moya Cannon

ACKNOWLEDGEMENTS

There are so many friends to be thanked here that I'm sure I'm going to exclude some, so first and foremost let me say thanks to you, the forgotten hero!

Thanks go on three levels: past, present and future. On the present level, my deepest gratitude goes to the people who directly co-shared this dream with me. Firstly, to Dom Kevin Healy, who in his usual meticulous style, carefully copied and scrutinised each note of the transcriptions. This he miraculously completed from the Benedictine monastery of Ewu-Ishan in Nigeria, working within the cracks of preparing the Nigerian Liturgical Calendar for 1997, ferrying people three days a week to hospital or carrying out his bursar responsibilities. I am so grateful to him for undertaking the scriptoria because, considering Fr Kevin's own musical and Gregorian Chant expertise, I wanted *nobody* else on this planet to do it, right from when the very first seed of this treasury was planted in my psyche! A small thank you to Mark Patrick Hederman, who gently and firmly encouraged the project with Kevin over a can of beer on a June evening in Nigeria a good few months ago! On the level of the present also, I must single out and name some other Benedictine monks from the Glenstal community. Firstly, Dom Placid Murray, who guided and grounded me from the beginning with presentation ideas, translations and above all, with a steady wisdom. Secondly, the librarians – Fr Vincent Ryan, Br Colman Clabby and Fr Mark Tierney – who unstintingly opened the doors wide for me. It is no accident that Glenstal Abbey still invigorates and heightens my perception of chant as a listener now at daily mass. The majority of chants here are Glenstal gems and I will be forever indebted to this wonderful community who over the years brought me so much closer to God and my deepest self.

Secondly, I will always remember and treasure the sharing and recording of these chants with the student priests of St Patrick's seminary, Thurles. Rev. Sean Fennelly I thank for being the 'glue' in the St Patrick's College connection. And within that connection, I will have to single out two people here: Kevin Muldoon, music director of the college, who was tremendously helpful, singing the chants with 'the lads' in between my visits, and all the time offering advice and expertise out of his own vast experience and musicianship; and cantor Paul Kelly, who worked on the ground, the perfect 'floor manager', rounding up the troops, setting up coffee, monitoring the politics and providing many special humorous as well as musical notes! To the eighteen other 'lads', I pray that your so important ministries ahead, wherever they may be, will be peacefilled and chantfilled.

Still in the present, this collection could never have been birthed without the help of Michael O'Brien and Íde ní Laoghaire of The O'Brien Press, who had the courage to 'grasp the publishing nettle'! To Íde, beside whom I stood for four years of our youth in Cór Cois Laoi singing our hearts and voices out, whether Gregorian Chant or not, I say *míle buíochas*. As an editor you were perfect, picking up on the 'clay feet' of this writer and enabling her heart to fly out of the unknown twilight!

On the past level, one of my earliest childhood memories takes me back to the church of the Benedictine Abbey of Glenstal where in the fifties my family in nearby Caherconlish would go for worship at Christmas and Easter, and I can still vaguely and fuzzily hear the very first sounds of chant in my ears. Twenty years later was to see me singing at a rural church opening celebration nearby in Caherline. On that day I sang my brand of plainchant then, which was *sean-nós*, at one side of the altar, and at the other, seven monks dotted the Mass with their Gregorian Chant. Dom Paul McDonnell, the cantor and organist there, casually invited me to sing at Glenstal the following Sunday, and the Glenstal bond began – a sacred bond, which apart from our recordings in the eighties, has taken flight many, many times for me when we entered a space through chant and prayer together. To Abbot Augustine O'Sullivan, Father Abbot then, I'm particularly grateful for his continuing consistent welcoming and warm supportive handshake, as indeed I am to Abbot Celestine Cullen and Abbot Christopher Dillon, who inherited me! In Irish, there is a term when one is requesting a song, and that is: *Cas amhrán dúinn*, 'turn us a song'. Well, to Brother Ciarán Forbes, who, over fourteen years, turned many a plainsong for me as sensitively as he turns his wooden bowls, thank you – especially for introducing me to my favourite chant of all time, 'Magnificat cum Alleluia'.

Preparing me, unknowingly, for this Glenstal bond during the sixties, the sisters of St Louis Convent, Dundalk, gave me my first hands-on, real taste and appreciation of Gregorian Chant. Three sisters in particular, two of whom are not with us now, come to mind. Sr Marie Renée, who gave me sufficient knowledge and love of Latin to be able to find my way around these texts; Mother Francis, who nurtured my singing. *Go ndéana Dia trócaire orthu, beirt.* And Sr Benedict, gentle musician and teacher, who awakened me to the whole cosmos of music and creativity. The seed sown by the St Louis sisters was carefully tended to by two people during the next decade of my life in college in the seventies: Pilib Ó Laoghaire, who had a huge feeling for and understanding not only of *sean-nós* singing but of the elusive, timeless movement of chant; and also Professor Aloys Fleischmann. Theory became practice during these university days when I would attend daily Mass and very often sing these chants in the indescribably beautiful ambience of the Honan Church, Cork. But that is all in the past.

Another community of sisters, the Cistercian sisters of St Mary's Abbey, Glencairn, County Waterford, have been an integral part of my life over the past five years. They share all my experiences and travels and love to hear all the details of what I'm up to. Sr Kate, the Latin scholar there, has translated several texts here. To Mother Abbess Agnes O'Shea and to the most affectionate, caring community in the world, I say thanks most of all for the prayers – and I know that they will genuinely be as excited about this book as I am!

On 26 September 1995, on the Feast of Saints Cosmos and Damien, as I walked home here to Dromore from Glenstal Mass, the notion of this compilation appeared. I quickly and enthusiastically typed up three pages. Having burdened it on the following people, I am thankful to you for replying and inspiring: Gerard Gillen and the National Advisory Music Board, Fr Tony Mullins, Fr Paddy Jones, Fr Eltin Griffin, Sean O'Boyle, Fr Seán Melody, Fr Liam Lawton and finally, Monsignor Seán Swayne, who died last year. Seán was always an inspiration and gentle, genuine support, and I'm sure he's somewhere up there leafing his way through this with you now.

Father Christy O'Dwyer, president of St Patrick's, was there in the background lending support and encouragement for us all. We sang these chants in the beautiful, powerful chapel space there, which enhanced the recording greatly. A final note of gratitude on the recording level must go to

Pearse Gilmore and Edel Ní Dhuinn of Xeric Studio, Limerick – two sensitive, talented, creative young people, who submitted graciously and patiently to this chant Baptism of Fire!

Collectively, I thank in alphabetical order, Moya Cannon, Sr Kathleen Deignan, Elinore Detiger, Allen Figgis, Jean Fitzgerald, Michael Fitzgerald, Rev. Austin Flannery OP, Sr Ann Flynn, O. Cist., Matthew Fox, Lynne Franks, Barbara Gaughen, Chantal Harris, Anjelica Huston, Brian Kennedy, Dr Brendan Kennelly, Agnes Kitto, Muriel McCarthy, Robert Muller, Sinéad O Connor, Stiofán Ó hAnnracháin, Gabriel Rosenstock, Tami Simon, Grace Smith, Suzanne Stephens, Karlheinz Stockhausen, Ann Thompson, Manec Van der Lugt, Dolores Whelan, Paul Winter.

Family always flavour strongly any inventive stew, and my two smashing sons, Micheál and Eoin, were often left 'in a stew' while I wrote and recorded! But after supper, dishtowels in hand, one washed and the other put away while 'Mud' ploughed on!

For every minute of every hour which I spent writing and singing, Evie, our West Highland terrier, sat under my chair, delighted at her captive audience, and in return contributed mountains of unspoken canine affection!

The future-looking side of this book concerns gratitude to you, the reader/listener, and that is ultimately the most important. Any artist and their history is only about the persons whom one meets and influences – and a singer/writer is so only because of the reader/listener. So this acknowledgement is to you.

Finally, above and beyond the past, present and future, I send my love to Micheál Ó Súilleabháin, who has lived with me as I sang and shared these chants throughout many years of very fertile struggles, and who, despite it all, still loves me.

SINGERS, ACCOMPANIMENTS, TRANSLATORS, QUOTATIONS

LIST OF SINGERS FROM ST PATRICK'S SEMINARY, THURLES

Kevin Muldoon, Musical Director of St Patrick's College, Thurles
Paul Kelly, Cantor and Soloist on 20, 22 and 26
Paul Bennet
Martin Blake
Rev. Brian Boyle
Gabriel Burke
Edward Daly
Richard Davern
Rev. Patrick Greene
T..J. Keane
Declan Kelly
Declan Kenny
Rev. Michael Leader
Mark Mohan
John Molloy
Cathal Murphy
Rev. Malachy Murphy
Rev. James O'Donoghue
Seamus O'Rourke
Gerard Ryan

ACCOMPANIMENTS

1	Agnus Dei XVIII	SURPETI
2	Alleluia	SURPETI
3	Attende Domine	SURPETI
4	Ave Maria	SHRUTI BOX
5	Ave Maris Stella	SURPETI
6	Ave Verum	SHRUTI BOX

7	Christe Redemptor Omnium	SURPETI
8	Concordi Laetitia	SURPETI
9	Credo III	SHRUTI BOX
10	Da Pacem Domine	SHRUTI BOX
11	Ecce Nomen Domini	SURPETI
12	Ego Sum	SHRUTI BOX
13	Gloria (Ambrosian)	SHRUTI BOX
14	Gloria (Missa de Angelis)	SHRUTI BOX
15	In Paradisum	SHRUTI BOX
16	Ite Missa Est	A CAPELLA
17	Jesu, Dulcis Memoria	SURPETI
18	Kyrie XVI	SHRUTI BOX
19	Kyrie XVIII	SHRUTI BOX
20	Lux Aeterna	A CAPELLA
21	Magnificat cum Alleluia	SURPETI
22	O Filii et Filiae	SHRUTI BOX
23	O Lux Beata Trinitas	SURPETI
24	O Pia Virgo	SURPETI
25	Pange Lingua	SHRUTI BOX
26	Pater Noster	SHRUTI BOX
27	Puer Natus in Bethlehem	SURPETI
28	Regina Caeli	SHRUTI BOX
29	Regnavit Dominus	SHRUTI BOX
30	Rorate Caeli	SURPETI
31	Salve Mater Misericordiae	SHRUTI BOX
32	Sanctus XVIII	SHRUTI BOX
33	Stabat Mater	SHRUTI BOX
34	Te Lucis Ante Terminum	SHRUTI BOX
35	Ubi Caritas	SHRUTI BOX
36	Veni, Sancte Spiritus	SHRUTI BOX
37	Veni, Veni, Emmanuel	SURPETI
38	Verbum Caro Factum Est	A CAPELLA
39	Victimae Paschali	SURPETI
40	Virgo Dei Genitrix	SURPETI

TRANSLATORS

To Sr Kate Cleary in St Mary's Abbey, Glencairn, I am deeply grateful for literal translations to the following nine chants: 'Attende Domine', 'Concordi Laetitia', 'Da Pacem Domine', 'Puer Natus in Bethlehem', 'Rorate Caeli', 'Salve Mater Misericordiae', 'Virgo Dei Genitrix'.

To Dom Placid Murray in Glenstal, my deepest gratitude not just for the literal translation of 'Ecce Nomen Domini', but for directing me towards many other sources which guided my own translations. The two most significant wellsprings here were: *Hymns of the Roman Liturgy* by Rev. Joseph Connelly (Longmans, London 1957) and *The Penguin Book of Latin Verse*, ed. Frederick Brittain (London, 1962).

BIBLIOGRAPHY

The book that says and tells it all is called *Western Plainchant*, published in 1993 by Oxford University and written by David Hiley, professor at the University of Regensburg.

In alphabetical order, here is a select general bibliography of the book-spring which inspired and nourished me:

Attwater, Donald, *The Penguin Dictionary of the Saints*, London, 1965

Civit, Isidro, G., *The Song of Salvation*, St Paul Publications, England, 1986

Dickinson, Emily, *The Complete Poems of Emily Dickinson*, edited by Thomas H. Johnson, Faber and Faber, London, 1970

Chetwynd, Tom, A *Dictionary of Symbols*, Paladin, London, 1982.

Fischer, Louis, *The Life of Mahatma Gandhi*, Grafton Books, London, 1951

Grout, J. and Palisca, C., A *History of Western Music*, Fourth ed., J. M. Dent, London, 1960

Kelly, A.A., ed, *Pillars of the House*, An anthology of verse by Irish Women, Wolfhound Press, Dublin, 1987

Heaney, Seamus and Hughes, Ted, eds., *The Rattle Bag*, Faber and Faber, London, 1982

McClellan, Randall, *The Healing Forces of Music*, Element Books, England, 1991

Martimort, A.G., ed., *The Church at Prayer: The Eucharist*; editors of English edition, Austin Flannery OP and Vincent Ryan OSB, Irish University Press, Shannon, 1971

Murphy, Gerard, *Ossianic Lore*, The Mercier Press, Cork, 1955

Murray, Patrick CSSp, ed., *The Deer's Cry*, Four Courts Press, England, 1986.

New Catholic Encyclopedia, The, Prepared by the Editorial Staff at the Catholic University of America, Washington, D.C., 1967

Ó hÓgáin, Dáithí, *Myth, Legend and Romance*, Ryan Publishing, London, 1990

Scholes, Percy, ed, *The Oxford Companion to Music*, Oxford University Press, London, 1974

Warner, Marina, *Alone of all her Sex*, Great Britain, 1976

CHRONOLOGY

A rough bird's eve view of the place in history of some of the chants. Dating these has largely been based on the texts; the tunes in many cases were wedded to the words much later.

1st century	Gospels of Matthew, Mark, Luke, John Revelation of John
4th century	O Lux Beata Trinitas, by St Ambrose, 334-397
6th century	Christe Redemptor Omnium
7th century	Te Lucis Ante Terminum Ave Maris Stella
8th century	Ubi Caritas, by Rufinus of Aquila, 796
10th century	Regina Caeli, attributed to Pope Gregory V, d. 999
11th century	Victimae Paschali, by Wipo, d.1048; Kyrie Eléison XVI (between 11th and 13th centuries)
12th century	Jesu, Dulcis Memoria Veni, Veni, Emmanuel Gloria (Ambrosian) Agnus Dei
13th century	O Pia Virgo, from Ludus Danielis (The Play of Daniel) Veni, Sancte Spiritus, by Stephen Langton, c.1150-1228 Sanctus XVIII Pange Lingua, by St. Thomas Aquinas, c.1225-1274
14th century	Stabat Mater Salve Mater Misericordiae Ave Verum
16th century	O Filii et Filiae, by Jean Tisserand, d.1494 Gloria (Missa de Angelis)
17th century	Credo III
19th century	Pange Lingua, tune first published in 1848 Puer Natus in Bethlehem 1886 MS

SOURCES

The following are the original sources from which I made the transcription: Cantus Marialis, Dom Potier, Paris 1903; Cantus Selecti; Glenstal Abbey repertoire; Graduale Romanum, 1949; Liber Cantualis, 1973; *Penguin Book of Latin Verse*, ed. Frederick Brittain, Penguin Books 1962; *Plainsong for Schools*, Society of St John Evangelist, Rushworth and Dreaper, Liverpool 1961. For extra verses and to see the original consult the following: Antiphonal Monasticum, Abbaye Saint-Pierre de Solesmes, Belgium 1934.

KEY

CM - Cantus Marialis
CS - Cantus Selecti
GL - Glenstal Abbey repertoire
GR - Graduale Romanum
LC - Liber Cantualis
Penguin - Penguin Book of Latin Verse
PSS - Plainsong for Schools

TITLE	SOURCE
1 Agnus Dei XVIII	GR p.768
2 Alleluia	LC p. 19 A, B, p.20 D
3 Attende Domine	CS p. 43
4 Ave Maria	CS p.112
5 Ave Maris Stella	CS p. 159
6 Ave Verum	CS p. 10
7 Christe Redemptor Omnium	AM p. 238
8 Concordi Laetitia	CM P. 73
9 Credo III	GR p. 774
10 Da Pacem Domine	LC p. 83
11 Ecce Nomen Domini	CS p. 33
12 Ego Sum	LC p. 61
13 Gloria (Ambrosian)	PSS
14 Gloria (Missa de Angelis)	GR p. 738
15 In Paradisum	LC p. 60

16 Ite Missa Est	LC 118
17 Jesu, Dulcis Memoria	LC p. 87
18 Kyrie XVI	GR p. 763
19 Kyrie XVIII (Missa de Profunctis)	GR p. 767 B
20 Lux Aeterna	LC p. 59
21 Magnificat cum Alleluia	CS p. 169
22 O Filii et Filiae	PSS
23 O Lux Beata Trinitas	AM p. 163
24 O Pia Virgo	CM P. 39
25 Pange Lingua	CS p. 270
26 Pater Noster	LC p. 27
27 Puer Natus in Bethlehem	CS p. 33
28 Regina Caeli	CS p. 133
29 Regnavit Dominus	GL
30 Rorate Caeli	CS p. 27
31 Salve Mater Misericordiae	CS p. 176
32 Sanctus XVIII	GR p. 767
33 Stabat Mater	CS p. 126
34 Te Lucis Ante Terminum	AM p. 171
35 Ubi Caritas	LC p. 108
36 Veni, Sancte Spiritus	LC p. 63
37 Veni, Veni, Emmanuel	Penguin
38 Verbum Caro Factum Est	LC p. 111
39 Victimae Paschali	LC p. 62
40 Virgo Dei Genitrix	CS p. 181

INDEX TO CHANTS